REALITY IS NEGOTIABLE

REALITY IS NEGOTIABLE

JUSTIN YARNELL

books that change your life

VANCOUVER, CANADA

First printing 2025

ISBN 978-1-897238-72-1

Library and Archives Canada Cataloguing in Publication

Title: Reality is negotiable : condensed milk for life / Justin Yarnell.

Names: Yarnell, Justin, author.

Identifiers: Canadiana (print) 20250101149 | Canadiana (ebook) 20250101262 | ISBN 9781897238721

(softcover) | ISBN 9781897238752 (EPUB)

Subjects: LCSH: Spirituality. | LCSH: Reality.

Classification: LCC BL624 .Y37 2025 | DDC 204—dc23

This book is meant to be informative, not prescriptive. The author of this book does not dispense medical advice nor prescribe the use of any technique or practice as a form of treatment for physical, mental, emotional, or medical problems, without the advice of a qualified physician, either directly or indirectly. The intent of the author is only to offer information of a general nature to help you in your quest for emotional and spiritual well-being. In the event that you use any of the information in this book for yourself or another, the author and the publisher assume no responsibility for your actions and their consequences.

PUBLISHED BY

NAMASTE PUBLISHING
Vancouver, BC, Canada
www.namastepublishing.com

Distributed in North America by: Ingram/Publisher's Group West
Original cover concept and art: Dayden Yarnell
Cover and interior book design: Mary Kellough

Printed in Canada on recycled paper by
FRIESENS CORPORATION

ALSO BY NAMASTE PUBLISHING

The Power of Now, Eckhart Tolle

A New Earth, Eckhart Tolle

Stillness Speaks, Eckhart Tolle

The Conscious Parent, Dr. Shefali Tsabary

Out of Control, Dr. Shefali Tsabary

Better Days, Neal Allen

The HOW to Inner Peace, Constance Kellough

The Presence Process, Michael Brown

Alchemy of the Heart, Michael Brown

The Revolutionary Trauma Release Process, Dr. David Berceli

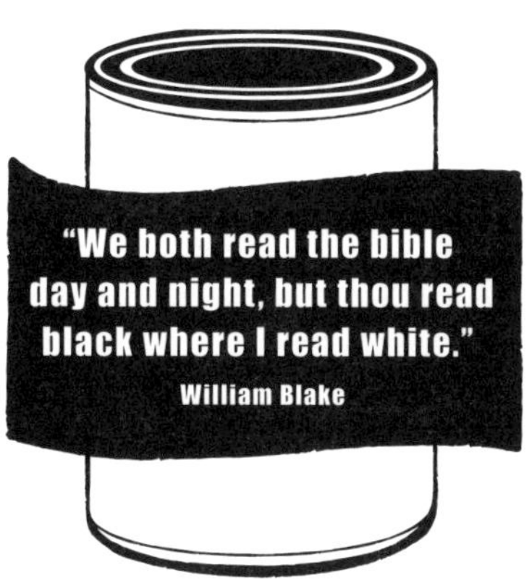
"We both read the bible day and night, but thou read black where I read white."
William Blake

This book is dedicated to

the woman in the white room; she goes by Tina.

TABLE OF CONTENTS

INTRODUCTION

Imagine yourself standing at the threshold of a softly glowing white room. How you got here, you don't know. In this room you are alone, except for a robed, faceless figure standing in front of you. This being is glowing slightly brighter than the room itself, almost blending in with its surroundings. You begin to hear this presence communicating with you, truth without words like you have never heard before. These truths are speaking to your soul because it's exactly what you've been longing for.

"Yes, yes," you say as the being imparts the universe's wisdom to you. You step closer because you are not afraid. As you approach, you see that where the figure's mouth would be is a portal swirling with the most beautiful colors you have ever seen. You gaze into the vacancy. Inside is infinite space, and all of eternity is before you. You are drawn to this but hesitant to let go of the world as you know it. *If I climb into the mouth of eternity, I may not return*, you think to yourself. It's like a vacuum, and you feel yourself being pulled.

At this time, a different being, a human man, enters the room. *It's now his turn to receive this truth*, you say to yourself.

The robed figure speaks aloud for the first time: "I have to go." You are saddened by this and don't want it to leave. It speaks one final time:

"Remember, it's like condensed milk."

The scene evaporates in front of you, and you find yourself standing in your living room, back in your normal 3D reality.

This is the origin story for the subtitle of this book, as experienced by my wife more than twenty years ago.

In the following pages, you will find the wisdom of the universe, the wisdom of God, and the wisdom of yourself in condensed form. Like actual condensed milk, it has been simmered and reduced down to its natural, nourishing sweetness. It is thick with ideas, truths, and practices that you, the reader, can blend in with your life—and in so doing, expand your consciousness and concept of yourself, which will provide a much more satisfying experience of reality.

The teachings and practices in this book have accumulated over lifetimes of spiritual seeking, presented here in condensed form with no unnecessary ingredients. How you read, practice, and apply them is entirely up to you. There is no "one way" to approach this book and no standards to uphold. Individual results may vary, but rest assured, you will get results.

We are all one, yet we are all unique individual expressions of the One. Approach this book in your own unique way, and simply do whatever feels right to you. If, while reading, a specific teaching seems to leap off the page and into your soul, pause there for a while and marinate in that experience. Some of these ideas may take some time to sink in, while others may just "click" the moment you encounter them. Either way, it's all good!

The Bible speaks of a "book of remembrance" (Malachi 3:16 KJV*). I believe this book is what we experience whenever we have an "Aha!" moment, a "lightbulb goes off," or we experience a revelation or "new" understanding. *We are simply remembering what we already know.* The information is actually nothing new; we have merely accessed a memory.

The intent of this collection of words that you now hold in your hands is to open the book of remembrance for you so that you will be able to start negotiating your day-to-day reality. Please realize that you already know everything written here, and the words contained within are simply meant to jog your memory.

*All Bible references in this book are taken from the King James Version (KJV) unless otherwise noted.

"If the doors of perception were cleansed, everything would appear to man as it is, infinite."

- William Blake

CHAPTER 1
REMEMBER WHEN

Reality is negotiable, and we are negotiating it all day long. However, most of us are completely unaware of this, and as a result, we think life is simply happening to us, when in reality, life is happening *through* us!

"Ye are the light of the world" (Matthew 5:14), and again, *"Ye are the salt of the earth"* (Matthew 5:13). We could just as easily say, "You are the life of the world!" You, me, we are life itself. We are animating the whole thing. We are giving life its flavor. We are creative, life-giving beings! At our core, we are the source of it all. We are the authors and the experiencers.

When we are born and open our eyes for the first time, we see a reality created by those who came before us. Everything we see was once only a thought in someone's imagination. Unaware of this, we perceive our surroundings as a concrete, fixed reality. If, however, we were born into a blank void, we would see the absolute malleability of our reality from the get-go. But since it doesn't happen this way, we learn early on (under false pretenses) that it requires intense physical effort to change things...and so the struggle of life begins.

For us to perceive that our reality is negotiable, we need to be in the appropriate state of mind. In spiritual circles, this state of mind is often referred to as Christ Consciousness. *"Let this mind be in you which was also in Christ Jesus: Who being in the form of God, thought it not robbery to be equal with God"* (Phil. 2:5-6), and again *"We have the mind of Christ"* (1 Cor. 2:16).

For us to have the mind of Christ, we need to be in the right state of being, and that state of being is God. You have to be Christ in order to have his mind. This is a tough one for many people. We are not robbing God of anything for us to consider ourselves equal with God, and if we are equal with God, then simply put, we are God. There is only one God. *"And Jesus answered him, the first of all commandments is, Hear, O Israel; the Lord our God is one Lord"* (Mark 12:29).

You, me, we = God.

I know many people struggle with this concept, but it is the truth. God became human so that we could become God.

We all may grow up with various religious backgrounds and ideas about who or what God is. Regardless of the variations, we all generally agree on three things: God is omnipotent (all powerful), God is omniscient (all knowing), and God is omnipresent (everywhere all the time). When you think about it, the only way these three things can be possible is if God is consciousness itself. This means that your very awareness of being is God, the I AM. You are the I AM. You may not have known this before now, but you have been God all along.

Surprise! You are God!

If this is a new concept for you, pause right here and sit still and quietly for a moment. Let the cares of the world fall away...and in the silence, you may hear a still, small voice from the depths of your inner being that whispers, "I AM." You can also ask in the silence, "Who is God?" and you may hear "I AM" from inside you. Try it for yourself. You have nothing to lose and a whole new identity to gain.

When you hear "I AM" this is God. This is also you.

We have a wonderful example of this in the book of Psalms. David speaks to himself (his higher Self speaks to his lower self), and he says, *"Be still and know I am God"* (Psalms 46:10). In this passage, David remembers who he is—he reminds himself of his divine nature.

This is something we all must do from time to time, because in this world where we live, and with the external-focused lives we lead, it's incredibly easy to get caught up in the drama of life and forget that we are God encased within these fleshly bodies. You can stay one step ahead in the game of life if you remind yourself of who you truly are at the start of each day!

The very fact that you are aware that you are alive proves that you are God. Jesus Christ, the man who physically embodied Christ Consciousness on Earth, says that we are all God. Read the Bible carefully and you are sure to understand this. Christ is not just "in your heart" as the church likes to teach, but he is you. So, *"let this mind be in you that was also in Christ Jesus!"* (Phil. 2:5).

Why is this reminder so important? You must be in the Christ state of being for reality to be negotiable.

Eighteenth century poet and visionary, William Blake said, "Both read the bible day and night, but thou read black where I read white." Over the centuries, we have taken the words and stories of the Bible and through various interpretations and misinterpretations, have created entire belief systems, social structures, mindsets, power dynamics and even war. We have also used the Bible as a source of comfort and inspiration, as a moral compass and as a portal to prayer.

The Bible is a powerful book. It is a book of reality creation.

It can be used to create a beautiful reality, and it can be used to create an ugly, hell-like reality depending on how it is interpreted.

The Bible can be interpreted on three distinct levels: The rock, the water, and the wine.

On the rock level, it is interpreted as a contradictory historical document—this is the level we base many of our laws upon. On the water level, it is alive and inspirational. On the wine level, it is a complete psychological drama filled with the high magic of reality creation, and on this level, it doesn't have a thing to do with secular human history. If we were to base our laws on the wine level, I believe it would usher in a new earth. The Bible is filled with all the power of now, and it is on this level that the verses shared in this book you are reading have been interpreted—the new wine.

This will likely require you to dispel most of your old views and beliefs about the Bible. You will have to shed many of your former preconceived notions of scripture in order to partake in the new wine. *"And no man putteth new wine into old bottles: else the new wine doth burst the bottles, and the wine is spilled, and the bottles will be marred: but new wine must be put into new bottles"* (Mark 2:22).

In the following pages, you will see that reality—your reality—is entirely negotiable. The caveat is you must remember that you are God. You may feel unprepared, with no training or skills to fulfill such a position. But, no worries, this hesitation stems solely from the mandatory process of incarnational forgetting. The Bible speaks of God *"making himself of no reputation"* (Phil. 2:7). In other words, he emptied himself, forgetting all prior knowledge that he was God in order to become fully human. It is the same with us. We have simply forgotten we are God.

We have all the knowledge of the universe inside of ourselves. Still, as we enter this human experience, as a prerequisite, we all must pass through the veil of forgetfulness, which allows us to have the full interactive human experience.

The following meditation can guide you into this new state of being, the state of being God, which is your natural state. Within this state of being, your memory will open, and you will be guided from one truth to the next as the glory of God is revealed in you.

MEMORY OF GOD MEDITATION
Duration: 30 min

Find a quiet place (if possible). Sit or lie down in a comfortable position and gently close your eyes. Take a slow, deep inhale through your nose, extending your abdomen with the breath. Hold the inhale for seven seconds. Then slowly exhale through your mouth. Repeat this six more times. Feel your body relaxing deeper and deeper with each slow breath. When thoughts arise, (and they will) simply acknowledge them and let them pass by like cars on the highway. Simply sit in the silence for seven minutes. Bring a slight smile to your face. In your mind, ask the question, "Who is God?" If an image of some version of God other than yourself comes to mind, simply acknowledge it, smile, and let it pass.

Oftentimes an image of God will reflect depictions we have seen in the past, such as a white-bearded male featured in the Sistine Chapel or a painting of Jesus with long flowing hair and blue eyes holding a lamb. This is perfectly normal and to be expected at first.

Continue sitting in the silence for another seven minutes. Then ask the question in your mind once more: "Who is God?" Picture the words "I AM" in your mind. Mentally say the words "I AM." Repeat the words "I AM" for the next seven minutes as a subtle mantra in your mind. When you are ready, begin to say it out loud, "I AM." Continue this for as long as it feels right to you. When you finish, smile and slowly open your eyes.

Like all the practices in the book, this meditation may require some time until you really feel it in the core of your being. This is natural, so don't be discouraged if you don't necessarily "feel" anything has changed. Eventually, you will. Often, changes are occuring that we are completely unaware of, but with practice, you will feel these changes unfurling within. You're right where you need to be!

"He whose face gives no light, shall never become a star."

\- William Blake

CHAPTER 2

WHY SO SERIOUS?

Reality is negotiable as long as you don't take life too seriously. Consider that when reality is taken seriously, it tends to harden into fixed patterns that become difficult to shape, escape, or negotiate.

If you are always serious, the mirror of life reflects seriousness back to you. Reality is revealed to us according to what state we are in.

Are you in a serious state? The mirror of life will reflect back serious situations to allow you to remain there. After all, reality is simply a reflection, nothing more, nothing less.

Do you know someone who is happy all the time, maybe so happy that the average person would find them annoying? Chances are they don't take life too seriously, They know that it is possible to take certain things in life seriously without entering into a state of seriousness ourselves.

The Bible says, *"A merry heart doeth good like a medicine"* (Proverbs 17:22).

What is medicine good for? To relieve symptoms? To heal? To make you feel better? Yes, all the above. So, if we are suffering from taking life too seriously, it is safe to say that we are ill, and if we are ill, we need some medicine. Interpreted at the level of wine, the Bible says that the medicine we need is a happy heart.

But how do we heal through a happy heart? First, remember that you are God. This concept is so vital, you will find this repeated throughout these pages. God doesn't take life too seriously. If you doubt this, take a look around. Observe the silly things we all do as humans. We can be ridiculous! Think of a time when you just had to stop and acknowledge how absurd life can be. We have all had those moments. Sometimes, the world can seem like one big cosmic joke, right?

If you know that you suffer from seriousness, there are many ways to seek out the medicine you need. The medicine itself is a merry heart. . We will first start with a small dose because this is usually all you need.

PRESCRIPTION #1 - SMALL DOSE

Duration: 10 Min

TAKE AS NEEDED

Sit comfortably in a quiet place (if possible). Take a deep slow breath. Relax as much as you can. Bring up the funniest or happiest memory you have. Hold it in your mind. Relive that memory by making it as real as possible. Bring all your senses into reexperiencing this memory—see the people and environment around you vividly, inhale the scents, feel the textures and nuances, recall the lightness in your heart. Allow yourself to smile. You can even laugh out loud with your eyes closed. Really feel it. You might even laugh so hard you cry. Keep laughing with your eyes closed as you replay the scene in your mind. Take another deep relaxing breath. Slowly open your eyes.

This is one of the most potent meditations you can do—the best part is, it's so easy!

Use this one as often as you wish throughout the day, especially if you've been dealing with something serious that blocks you from holding happiness in your heart. It's good medicine!

The next method is a much larger dose. It is intended for those who suffer from more extreme seriousness.

PRESCRIPTION #2 - LARGE DOSE

Duration: Varies

TAKE ONCE AND REPEAT EVERY SIX MONTHS IF NEEDED

It is time to get brutally honest with yourself—I mean pure, raw, unfiltered honesty. Grab a notebook or several pieces of paper along with a pen or pencil. Now, write down every trauma and tragic event that has ever happened to you. This may sound daunting but just take your time. Write down everything you can think of. If it's only one major thing, that's fine. If it's several major things, that's fine too. As you are writing this down, there may be moments that are difficult to bear. Let me assure you, the pain and struggle will be worth it. Cry if you need to. Get angry if that helps. You are pulling all of these disappointments and betrayals up and out of your innermost being, bringing them into the space of the present. This is brave work, and you are courageous to do it. This process may take you ten minutes, or it may take you several days—whatever it takes, please do this for yourself. Get it all out and written down on paper.

Once this is completed, read over everything you have written. Acknowledge every emotion that surfaces and allow yourself to feel all the way through it without stifling your response the way you have for a lifetime. Once you have purged these tragic and traumatic experiences and written them down, place your hand over your heart and extend gratitude and love towards yourself. Allow yourself to recognize that in spite of all these negative experiences, you are still here. You are still standing. You are remarkable—a resilient miracle.

Now, take your paper and safely burn it. As you watch the edges curl in the flames and blue smoke rise as the paper burns to ash, realize and understand that all this negativity is now out of you. It's gone. It has been burned away. During this time, forgive everyone who was involved in those events. Also forgive yourself. Let them go...let it all go. As you stare at the ashes, understand that you are now free. Released by the chains and memories of the past, you are free. This freedom is your new state of being.

This is an extremely powerful cleansing ritual that produces profound results. It serves as a reset button for your life and creates a merry heart because you are returning to your natural state, which is one of freedom and happiness. *"Weeping may endure for a night, but joy cometh in the morning"* (Psalms 30:5). *"These things have I spoken unto you, that my joy may remain in you, and that your joy might be full"* (John 15:11).

"What is now proved was once only imagined."

- William Blake

CHAPTER 3
PURE IMAGINATION

The universe is mental, reality is mental. All is mental. Thoughts become physical reality. As Willy Wonka once sang, "We're living in a world of pure imagination."

Think about it for a minute. Look around you right now and observe your immediate surroundings. Everything you see was once just a thought in someone's imagination. The couch, the table, the TV, the car, your computer, your clothes, your food, even this book you are reading right now. All of this was once only a thought in someone's head—thoughts upon thoughts.

People are free to use their imagination for all things, good, bad, or indifferent. This is what we read in the Bible , *"See now that I, even I, am he, and there is no god with me: I kill, and I make alive; I wound, and I heal: neither is there any that can deliver out of my hand"* (Deut. 32:39). It is all God, good or bad, and it is all you. We can imagine good things for ourselves and others or bad things for ourselves and others. It is totally up to us. The Bible says, *"For as he thinketh in his heart, so is he"* (Proverbs 23:7).

How do you think about yourself? It's a simple yet important question to ask. Can you imagine right now the man or woman you want to be? What are you like? What are your hobbies? How do you feel? What kind of thoughts do you have? What about your daily routines? How do you dress? How do you carry yourself? Are you friendly and outgoing? How about the music you listen to? What TV shows and movies are you into? What kind of books do you read? How do you talk, and what kind of food do you eat?

Now realize that you can actually step into that role you envision. Take the time to imagine you as your ideal self right now! Imagine the person you would like to be. Grab a piece of paper and a pen, and quickly write everything you can visualize about this version of you. Ask yourself all the above questions and write down the answers as they come to you in a stream of consciousness. Do not stop or edit your responses. Once you have written down all the attributes of the ideal version of yourself, pick two and start implementing them today. You can do that right now! As the days go on, start "being" this version of yourself. Start with the easy ones, the ones that are immediately attainable. Eat something different for dinner tonight. Read a new book. Get a haircut if you want to change your appearance. Slowly but surely, start becoming the person you want to be. This is a powerful way to change your reality. As you start being who you want to be, the mirror of life reflects the new you in your new reality. You see, the universe doesn't give us what we want—it gives us what we are.

It's important to keep in mind that although we are all one, we are all unique expressions of the One, and so we all have different ideas of who we would like to be. There are no right or wrong answers here. Whatever you can imagine yourself being, you can be. There's one caveat: whatever you imagine yourself being must be plausible to you. There should be an ease, a naturalness about this way of being—as if somehow it was always deep down inside of you.

This is how reality is created.

Since art often imitates reality, let's take a quick look at Mark Twain's classic *The Prince and the Pauper*, which illustrates this idea beautifully. Set in the 1500's, a young boy named Tom Canty is growing up on the wrong side of the tracks in London, England. He lives in a ramshackle house with his abusive father and abusive grandmother, and they both abuse him and belittle him daily. Tom doesn't like his environment and knows he deserves better. One night, he begins to use his imagination. He begins to see himself living in a positive, upper class, loving environment. He imagines he lives on the other side of the tracks, living amongst the royal families in London. Despite his current undesired physical reality, he begins to act differently. He begins to think differently and see himself as he desires to be.

Tom uses his imagination daily, seeing himself as his ideal version. As the story goes on, Tom begins to hold his head higher; he starts to feel himself to be who he desires to be. He begins to speak positively about himself, and he eventually ends up living with the royal family in a place of honor.

What's so special about Twain's story is that this is how reality creation works. You see the ideal version of yourself, and you begin to act like it, speak like it, and most importantly, feel like it. This is the difference between imagination and mere fantasy: the *feeling*.

Everybody can use their imagination to picture anything they wish. But when you use your imagination with the intention to create a new reality for yourself, and you can begin to *feel* it, that's when the magic happens. When it begins to feel natural and real to you, then you will experience it in your physical reality. People habitually say, "I'll believe it when I see it," but that's backward thinking. We should be saying, "I'll believe it, then I'll see it."

There is a difference between intentional imagination and fantasy. For a guy like me in his mid-40s, if I were to imagine that I am a pro-NFL Quarterback (with no previous football experience), I simply could not do it. That would be merely fantasy football. I could never imagine it to the point of feeling it like a reality, at least not at this stage along my journey of enlightenment. If I were an Ascended Master, maybe, but I think it's safe to say that most of us aren't quite there.

Being a pro-NFL Quarterback lies beyond my field of perception. I can dream about it and fantasize about it all day long, but I simply cannot truly see myself consciously becoming it to a point where it feels natural. It's like this: we could close our eyes and imagine riding on a fire-breathing dragon through the clouds, but that's just fantasy; we're not intentionally trying to manifest the reality of riding on a dragon.

Let me share an example from my life regarding this idea. Several years ago, I was in a sad state. I was recently divorced after 18 years of marriage with four kids. I was drinking daily to try and numb out the world. I was the opposite of the Pink Floyd song...I was "uncomfortably numb." I was essentially broke, hitting rock bottom as I made one poor decision after another.

Honestly, I was ashamed of myself. Looking back now, life was reflecting exactly who I was being, and that's all it can do because our external reality is a mirror. I was as low as I could get, barely able to keep food on the table for my kids.

On a day off, I decided to walk to the local public library. I strolled around the crowded stacks looking for something new to read and stumbled upon the book, *Breaking the Habit of Being Yourself - How to Lose Your Mind and Create a New One*, by Dr. Joe Dispenza. I had no idea what this book was about, but it piqued my curiosity.

Little did I know, my life was about to change.

Breaking the Habit of Being Yourself describes the neurological changes that occur in your brain when you begin to change the way you think about yourself. He explained in very easy-to-understand terms that "your personality creates your personal reality" and that it is possible to change your life by changing your mind.

I read through that entire book twice and practiced the meditations day in and day out. I eliminated old ways of thinking and started seeing myself in a new light. I learned a fundamental lesson: *when you change the way you look at things, the things you look at change.*

As the things I was looking at began to change, new opportunities appeared in my reality. I crossed paths with a friend I hadn't seen in years. He owned a large landscaping company and offered me a job with better hours and more pay. It was a true blessing. Things were starting to change.

After I had been working this new job for several months, one day my owner friend looked at me. Out of nowhere he said, "You're pretty good at this. I don't know why you don't start your own business." That hit me like a ton of bricks. Why hadn't I ever thought about that before?

Good question. I'll tell you why. Starting my own business had never even entered my mind, because my old way of thinking simply wouldn't allow it. However, I was changing my thoughts about myself, and that mental shift brought about a physical change in my reality.

After that moment of awakening, my friend ended up helping me start my own landscaping business. He gave me several customers to start out with, helped me build a website, and gathered all the equipment I would need. I was able to set my own schedule, spend more time with my family, and provide for them in the ways I had always wanted.

This experience taught me a fantastic lesson about the subconscious law of reality creation. I learned that when the universe presents you with an opportunity to evolve, contained within that opportunity are all the necessary things needed for its fulfillment. This is true every single time.

As your field of perception expands (from changing your thoughts), new opportunities naturally begin to show up, and all you have to do is step into them. You can trust the universe on this one—it always has your back. The universe itself is always evolving and expanding, and its goal is to get you to evolve and expand along with it. This is because you are an integral part of it. Ever interconnected, as one expands and evolves, so does the other.

Our imagination can and should be used at every stage of life. Do you remember being a kid with an active imagination? Most kids have no problem going into their imagination, it just comes natural to them, but for some reason as we get older, we tend not to use it all that much as adults; however, your imagination (which is a beautiful aspect of the Christ) will *"never leave thee nor forsake thee"* (Hebrews 13:5). It's always right there, ready and willing to create your desires. The issue is that, when we're not actively involved, consciously using our imagination to negotiate a happy reality, the same old thought patterns keep creating the same old things. Same bad stuff, different day.

The name of the game is Make-Believe. You need to make yourself believe that you are the ideal version of yourself living your best life. How do you do this? By using your imagination to see yourself as you want to be. When you believe the best for yourself, your subconscious mind accepts it as truth and creates your reality to match your belief. Start playing Make-Believe and watch what happens.

The Bible says, *"...Except ye become as little children, ye shall not enter into the kingdom of Heaven"* (Matthew 18:3). So, where is this Kingdom of Heaven, and what is it? We see in the Bible (Luke 17:21) *"For behold, the Kingdom of God is within you."* The Kingdom of Heaven and the Kingdom of God are one and the same, and this is your wonderful human imagination. Here, we are told that we need to be like little children to enter the Kingdom, and little children are always actively using their imaginations.

Here is another secret!

Your life can be heaven or hell depending on how active you are in your own imagination. Why not decide right now to become actively involved in your imagination (creating with intention), lighten up, play Make-Believe like a child, and enter the Kingdom of Heaven?

ACTIVE IMAGINATION MEDITATION
Duration: 20 min

Sit or lie down in a comfortable position. Inhale slowly and deeply through your nose and slowly exhale through the mouth. Repeat this seven times. Try to relax as fully as possible. Sometimes it helps to exhale the final breath with a sigh. Bring into your imagination the ideal version of yourself. Imagine your ideal weight, hairstyle, and clothing. Visualize yourself as fully as you can. Better yet, *feel* yourself. Feel the vision in your physical body. This is equally as effective.

The important thing here is to stay relaxed and lighthearted because Make-Believe is supposed to be fun! Bring a smile to your face as you see and feel this ideal version of yourself.

Now, picture something that you would like to accomplish, something that would make you feel amazing if it were true. Try to see through the eyes of this version of yourself...it is you, after all! Do the best you can to visualize yourself accomplishing that thing. Feel this sense of accomplishment as a warm feeling of relief settling into your body. Rest in this feeling for at least two minutes, or longer if you wish (whatever feels right for you). Now, slowly, very slowly, open your eyes.

When we can conjure the feeling of an event before it has happened in our 3D reality, if we can really feel what it feels like, the mirror of life begins to reflect circumstances and events that match that feeling. The subconscious mind does not know the difference between a real and an imagined event. It creates reality based on what we believe to be true, and when you believe something to be true, you can feel it.

When we think good thoughts, we feel good in our bodies. This is why the Bible says, *"Finally, brethren, whatsoever things are true, whatsoever things are honest, whatsoever things are just, whatsoever things are pure, whatsoever things are lovely, whatsoever things are of good report; if there be any virtue, and if there be any praise, think on these things"* (Phil. 4:8).

If you can get into the habit of thinking lovely thoughts for yourself and others right now, then you really have no need to worry or even think about what may or may not happen in the future. *"Take therefore no thought for the morrow: for tomorrow will take thought for the things of itself"* (Matthew 6:34).

If you can feel happy and excited now, in the present moment, then you've got this! No matter what time or day it is, you will only ever experience it in the present moment.

Do you ever wonder where yesterday went or where tomorrow comes from? No, because there is only the now, and whenever the "future" arrives it will always be experienced "now."

"Love to faults is always blind, always is to joy inclined. Lawless, winged and unconfined, and breaks all chains from every mind."

- William Blake

CHAPTER 4

WHAT'S LOVE GOT TO DO WITH IT?

You are God, I am God, we are God, and *"God is love"* (1 John 4:8).

Whether we know it or not, our natural state of being is one saturated with love. Throughout life, we learn to create mental smog for ourselves. We use words and phrases such as "falling in love" because it indicates that we appear to be out of love. Except, that is impossible. "*...Neither death, nor life, nor angels, nor principalities, nor powers, nor things present, nor things to come, nor height, nor depth, nor any other creature, shall be able to separate us from the love of God, which is in Christ Jesus"* (Romans 8:38-39)

Oftentimes, we feel like we're not "in love" because of our innate human dualistic viewpoint. We tend to see everything and everyone in our reality as being separate from ourselves; when in fact, we are all one.

Underneath the appearance of individuality, underneath our personal concept of ourselves, we are all the same eternal, formless consciousness that is God. Think about the fact that we live on a giant rock spinning around in outer space. All of us are here. All of us were born here. We were literally born in outer space!

We are truly part of the planet, a piece of the cosmos. We are of the cosmos because we were created in and from there, so we are all part of this same origin of life and the universe. We are not "separate" from anything—not from each other, not from nature, not from the world, not from distant stars with their own galaxies rotating around them.

We are the world. Are you of an age to remember that song from 1985? It was more accurate than we thought! As the Christian mystic Neville Goddard once said, "The entire universe is simply yourself pushed out."

Most people seem to assume that God is something separate, some entity residing elsewhere in a separate location; and typically this is due to the Church's teaching of duality throughout the centuries. Many of us grew up being taught that we can break our fellowship with God. I hope you'll discover in this book that this possibility is impossible.

When we see God as something separate from ourselves, we are opening our minds to a life filled with condemnation and confusion. As *if* Jesus Christ is someone that you have to "ask into your heart"! Ludicrous. Total nonsense! God is your very awareness of being, your consciousness, your own wonderful human imagination. Why would you ever need to ask yourself into your own heart?

God is love; you are God—therefore, you are love.

The false belief in dualism and separation is dangerous because of its multifaceted nature. Not only can dualism result in our belief that God is something separate from us, but also that we, as human beings, are separate from each other. Because of biblical misinterpretation of the scriptures, a line is drawn in the metaphorical sand within the Church itself. Certain groups of people then decide that they are the only ones who have it right. It's our way or the highway to hell.

Separation starts at the top of the belief system and trickles down to all the other levels, causing more ripples of separation wherever it goes. This is why we see so many different denominations within the "Christian" Church. All sects believe in God, but that tends to be where the concept of oneness stops.

Each set of beliefs splinters off and creates another subset of beliefs. Certain groups are absolutely certain that they are the only ones going to heaven and anyone who believes differently than them is considered "lost." It is really sad when this group-think mentality sets in and becomes a way of life. People who believe in God look down on other people who also believe in God, often in disgust, simply because they believe slightly differently than they do. This happens within the Christian Church all the time, and it extends outside of the Church as well; eventually, all religions except your own are considered wrong. Why can't we understand that multiple religions can be right and true?

What do we know about love? *"Love is patient, love is kind. It does not envy, it does not boast, it is not proud. It does not dishonor others, it is not self-seeking, it is not easily angered, it keeps no record of wrongs. Love does not delight in evil, but rejoices with the truth. It always protects, always trusts, always hopes, always perseveres. Love never fails..."* (1 Cor. 13:4-8 NIV).

Here, we see what love does and doesn't do. It's all contained right there. The entire universe of which you are a part is love from beginning to end.

Your life is love from beginning to end. You are the Alpha and the Omega and everything in between.

So, who are you? You are love. You are patient, you are kind, you are truthful. You are protected, you are trusting, you are hopeful, and you are persevering. It's easy to look at this list of attributes and say to yourself, "That's not me! I'm not very patient, I'm not very trusting," and so on. The truth is you are! This is your true nature. The truth is you *are* loving, patient, kind, truthful and trusting. These qualities are built into you, and you can't get away from them. If we don't know these truths about ourselves, then it becomes very difficult to live an authentic love-filled life.

Our reality mirrors our awareness as well as our unawareness. If you are not aware that you have all these wonderful qualities, your reality reflects situations and circumstances to match your unawareness. In this situation, ignorance is not bliss!

For instance, if you are not aware that you have patience, your reality will reflect situations and circumstances that cause you to be impatient all the time; you'll always be in a hurry, always agitated. Once again, the cause of this is our dualistic viewpoint of God being something separate from ourselves. This is why it appears that society as a whole is impatient and obsessed with making things faster; it seems as if we simply can't tolerate waiting for anything. We are unaware that we are love, and love is patient.

I went out to eat at a restaurant in South Florida. It seemed like it took forever for the waiter to take our order, and when he finally did, it seemed like it took an eternity for him to bring us our drinks. Once they finally arrived, it seemed like forever had passed before we finally got our food.

The people I was with noticed that I wasn't used to this, and just smiled and said, "You're on island time now." I realized right then that the purpose of my experience was all about slowing down, talking with my friends and family, feeling the sand beneath my toes, and breathing in the salty air while I watched the sunset over the ocean. The point was to be in the beautiful present moment.

Reality is negotiable when we slow down, quiet the wheels of the mind, and relax. Just be. In Love. With Life.

We had a wonderful time that night on Island time, but reality is negotiable. We could have altered it by complaining about the slow service, and that would have changed everything. It would have ruined the whole vibe and cast a gloominess over ourselves and the waiter. It could have turned out completely differently if we'd decided we wanted to rush the experience, which would have caused a negative memory for years to come.

This simple story illustrates that reality is negotiable all the time, every second of every minute of every day. Most of us are not aware of this. Most of us think that reality is happening to us rather than through us. Everything changes when you start creating reality with intent and with the awareness that you are God.

This whole life thing is about being in love. Just being. So, how do we "be" in love?

One easy and practical way to live your life being in love is to recognize the attributes of love: Love is patient, kind, not envious, not boastful, not proud, not dishonoring, not self-seeking, not easily angered, doesn't keep records of wrongdoing, does not delight in evil, tells the truth, protects, trusts, hopes, perseveres. Look at this list, pick one or two things and begin to cultivate them in your daily life. The idea here is to truly feel and be these things. There's no rush and no pressure whatsoever. We have all the time in the world to do this, so just start with one thing. Besides, time doesn't really exist anyway—it's always the present moment, no matter what.

We are all one, yet in many forms. Some of us may be strong in one area of love and weak in another. Some of us may be strong in all areas of love, and some of us may be weak in all areas of love. No judgment, we're all in this together! Love rejoices in truth, so right now we need to be truthful with ourselves about our strengths and weaknesses when it comes to love. Look over the list again and be honest with yourself. Find one of these areas that you know you could improve upon. Let this be your intention for the next few days to cultivate your chosen qualities.

The more you cultivate the qualities of love, the more your reality becomes negotiable.

Let's look at envy for example. We've all experienced it. Maybe one of our coworkers gets a promotion, and we feel like we should have been the one to get it; we experience envy. Maybe someone we know finds the love of their life, and we haven't met ours yet; we feel envious of them. Maybe you're looking at social media, and it seems like everyone you know is taking permanent luxury vacations (which they're probably not in reality, lol) and we're envious wondering why our life isn't that easy. Let's make it our goal this week, then, when we see or hear of someone else receiving something we ourselves would like to receive, instead of envy we try to feel genuine happiness for them. I know it's not always easy, but a fun way to do this is to imagine ourselves in their shoes, imagine you are them (because in truth, you are) and try to feel real gratitude on their behalf. This is actually enjoyable, and it provides a wonderful distraction for the ego for the time being, which is always a good thing!

When you can feel gratitude for someone else, it's the same as feeling gratitude for yourself, and gratitude is the optimum state of receivership. When you can be grateful for someone else's life experience, you draw a similar experience to yourself. It's part of the golden rule, do unto others as you would have them do unto you.

Practice makes perfect.

How can you cultivate patience? How can you practice not being easily angered? How can you practice not holding grudges? How can you practice not bragging? How can you practice being trusting? How can you practice being hopeful? How can you practice not being self-seeking? How can you practice perseverance?

This is the real work, the foundation of reality creation. The plan is to take it one at a time, and master that one. How do you know when you've mastered it? You will know that you have mastered it when you really feel it. *"Not just in words, but in deeds (feels) also"* (1 John 3:18). This is how affirmations work—you have to feel them. It won't really do you any good to walk around saying "I am patient" if you don't feel patient. The *feeling* is the secret.

The next time someone does or says something that makes you angry, use the opportunity to transcend the anger and conquer it. Love conquers all. Seeing these instances as the opportunities that they are, we begin to perceive life as a game of awakening to who we truly are. As we begin to cultivate the different aspects of love, we "power up" and advance to higher levels. The universe is always advancing, and when you can see your daily life in this way, it becomes fun, and you start looking at the challenges of life as opportunities to awaken and advance to deeper levels of your true self.

Love is the most magical thing in the world, and the more we are aware of it, the more powerful our lives become. Love is the magical currency of the spiritual world. The Bible speaks of this when it says, *"Love never fails"* (1 Cor. 13:8 NIV) and *"Love covers over a multitude of sins"* (1 Peter 4:8 NIV).

To interpret these verses at the level of new wine, we must first loosen our grip on what our concept of sin is. The idea of sin is probably the most misunderstood thing in all of scripture, and this misunderstanding runs deep! Thanks to the teachings of the Church, we all seem to have this embedded belief that sin is something God punishes us for, but nothing could be further from the truth. I like how Elbert Hubbard said, "We are not punished for our sins, we are punished by our sins."

So, let's break this down just a bit further. In the Old Testament, the Hebrew word *cheit*, commonly translated as sin, literally means "to miss the mark." Imagine you are shooting a bow and arrow, and you don't quite hit the bullseye. That's all it means. It doesn't have a thing in the world to do with punishment from some all-seeing vengeful God. We are aiming at something, and we don't quite hit it, that's sin.

As another example, you're having a discussion with your spouse, and you have different opinions about what color to paint the kitchen. She thinks yellow would look nice (and she's probably right) but you believe egg-shell white would look even better. You certainly were not planning on it, but this simple conversation turns into an argument, and you both end up saying things you should not have said to each other. You missed the mark, you were aiming at coming to a mutual decision about the paint color, and...well, you didn't. A little time goes by, and you feel bad about the things you said, and the whole rest of the day just doesn't feel right; the whole vibe is tainted. That's being punished by your sins. It has nothing to do with a God up in Heaven keeping track of all your wrongdoings. Even if there was some secular being up there, they wouldn't be keeping tabs on all your sins, because God is love, and love keeps no record of wrongs, remember?

I know so many people who go through life constantly feeling guilt and condemnation. They believe that they have sinned against God. They spend their life in a perpetual state of repentance, believing that we are "all just sinners saved by grace." Ever heard of that one?

At this point, we might as well clear up the universal misunderstanding of the word "repent" as well. In the New Testament, which was originally written in Greek, *metanoia* is the Greek word for *repentance*. The word "repent" literally means "to change your mind." It's not about begging some external God for forgiveness. Thanks again to the Church, many people all over the world take this word to extreme measures. Not only do they feel guilt and shame, but many feel like they have to punish or deny themselves because of it. When I was in India several years ago, I saw people walking barefoot over broken glass while whipping themselves with leather straps because they sincerely believed that's what they had to do to repent of their sins.

In the West, most people don't employ physical means of repentance, such as walking on broken glass; however, many here do, in fact, punish themselves mentally with feelings of unworthiness, guilt, and shame. It's a horrendous way to live when you constantly feel like you're not good enough to live up to the standard set by a perfect, fault-finding God.

Let's refer back to our example of painting the kitchen. After a little time goes by, you both feel remorse for acting badly, you apologize to each other, and then you have a romantic make-up. You both obviously opened your minds to your different opinions on the paint color and worked it out. Yellow it is! Now that's true repentance!

Love is more powerful than anything we could ever say or do. The formless consciousness beneath all our egos is God, and God is love.

Religious organizations that teach sin as something punishable by God inevitably create that reality for themselves and their followers. This forces them to come up with dogmatic rules that rob them of their personal freedom. These rules and regulations are of course impossible to follow, causing and even encouraging outrageous and oftentimes unlawful behavior, such as sexual abuse against children. Trying to avoid an eternal hell, they create hell on Earth for themselves and their congregations. But this is a chapter on love, not sin, so we don't need to focus on it too much. However, to have a strong awareness of love, we needed to address the issue. As our awareness of reality expands, reality becomes more negotiable.

Love Wins is the title of a book by Rob Bell, and it served as one of the turning points along my personal spiritual path. There is no hell because God is love, and love wins. That was the general message. Like me, Bell had spent his life in Christian ministry; unlike me, at one point he was the Senior Pastor of one of America's largest churches. His awareness of love changed his thinking, which changed his beliefs, which changed his life.

At the time *Love Wins* was published, I had been in Christian ministry for over 20 years but had recently resigned from my full-time position at a megachurch in Oklahoma—a church I had been involved with for the previous 10 years—so this book met me right where I was at. I had already been contemplating the idea that there was no literal place called hell, where we are eternally separated from our loving God. This book resonated with me like the way thunder shakes the ground, and it made some pretty big waves throughout the Church community. Bell was considered a heretic by many highly successful pastors and their flocks. How dare he suggest something so awful as there is no hell?

Many people simply can't imagine a gospel without a hell, but the real question is, how could you imagine a gospel with one? The word "gospel" means "good news," and this message of love without a place of eternal suffering in a lake of fire sounds pretty good to me.

"And ye shall know the truth, and the truth shall make you free" (John 8:32). The fact that there is no hell is one of the first central truths that set me free from a lifetime of false beliefs.

I was excited and eager to share this message with people because it truly changed my life; however, as I began to tell people that I no longer believed in a place called hell, I started to realize that there are a ton of people out there who just don't want to be set free, at least not yet. The truth had flung my prison gates wide open, but they wanted to stay within the walls of false religious beliefs...and you know, that's perfectly alright. They will eventually know the truth and be set free. Love endures forever, and nothing—not even deeply rooted false beliefs—can outlast it.

Even if you don't interpret the Bible on the level of new wine, and you still see it as a literal historical text, the idea of a hell just doesn't jive. On the lowest level of biblical interpretation, the rock level, one would see God as a separate entity, and that entity would be the everlasting father, and we, his children. Now, those of you who have children, you love them, right? Is there anything your children could possibly do to cause them not to be your children anymore? Is there anything that they could say or do to cause you to torture them for all of eternity? Even if they came to you and told you that they no longer believed in you as their parent, it doesn't change the fact that they're still your children, right? It would be hurtful to hear them say something like that, but they're still your children no matter what, and you still love them, regardless of their actions.

Now, imagine if you will, a father here in our normal everyday physical reality. He tells his children that he loves them, but he also tells them that if they don't believe in him and obey his every word, that he is going to torture them for the rest of their lives, and then forever and ever. Undoubtedly, this man would be immediately apprehended, and thrown into prison for threatening his children like that. Do you see how crazy this is?

Imagine that you tell your significant other that you love them forever and you want them to love you back, but if they don't, you're going to beat them into submission? What kind of a relationship would that be?

As above, so below. If our current earthly, physical reality and modern laws don't condone or allow that type of behavior, then it's safe to say that it's not allowed or supported in the spiritual realm either.

Our awareness of love should continually expand like the entire universe is expanding right now as you read this. When we dissolve our limiting beliefs, a spontaneous expansion of consciousness occurs, and the more we learn about love, the more we learn about ourselves.

As your awareness of love expands to a certain point, something fabulously peculiar happens. When and how this happens seems to vary from person to person, but I have spoken to enough people to know that it is a sure thing. I call it an organic eruption of infinite love. This first happened to me years ago when I was out doing some landscaping for one of my clients. Suddenly, I was enveloped by the most brilliant glowing golden light. It was incredibly loving and warm, and it saturated my entire being. I was instantly overwhelmed with the feeling of "being in love" like I had never experienced before. It was a feeling of being in love with the entire universe and everything within it, and it was reciprocal because I could feel the love the universe had for me as well, similar to that magical and obsessive passion you feel for someone at the start of a relationship. It was like that but multiplied by a million.

It was coming from deep inside of me. I felt the source of infinite love in the core of my being. It was almost unbearable; I felt like I was going to explode or lose consciousness right there on the spot. I began to weep, standing there in my client's front yard surrounded by lawn equipment. I must have been a sight to see!

Right there, in that moment, I knew I was God. Not in the David Koresh weird cult type of way, but in a way where I was suddenly aware that we, all of us, make up this thing we call God. I was feeling, for the first time, the raw and unfiltered power of unconditional love.

I sat down on the grass for fear of passing out if the feeling became more substantial. As I sat there weeping uncontrollably, a still small voice from within whispered, "You are the Big Bang." In this magical moment, I instinctively knew that this was what had started it all: a spontaneous, organic eruption of pure love. One super-condensed ball of eternal love exploded into infinite versions and varieties of itself. The Big Bang. It's you, it's me, it's we...and we're still banging.

After several minutes passed and the tears started to recede, I began to feel another peculiar feeling that I had never experienced before; it was at once entirely lovely and yet entirely lonely at the same time. I knew at that moment that there was no separate being, no outside God that I could pray to for help, but that it was inside me. It was me, and I was it—everything and yet nothing.

This feeling, I now know, was the loneliness of being in the void. Another influential teacher, Ram Dass, spoke about this feeling in many of his public lectures in the 60s and 70s. It is a feeling that can only be understood by reading the first paragraph of Genesis at the very beginning of the Bible: *"And the earth was without form and void; and darkness was upon the face of the deep. And the Spirit of God moved upon the face of the waters"* (Genesis 1:2). That was us, as one, hovering over the formless void. We are still one, we have simply multiplied, and when we go deep within, to the formless consciousness that we all are, we merge with God, our true selves.

As this feeling started to fade, it metamorphosed into a sense of ultimate oneness. Everything is one, only one. Alone yes, but not singular. We are all just fragments of the one, and each fragment is simultaneously a part of and contains the whole. Each one of us is simply a different and unique viewpoint of God. As spiritual teacher Ram Dass, once said, "We're all just God in drag."

SACRED HEART BREATH MEDITATION
Duration: 20 Minutes

Find a quiet and comfortable place (if possible), a chair with a back works best. Sit up straight with your feet flat on the floor. Breathe slowly and deeply into your chest, visualizing the breath coming into your heart.

Imagine all people, imagine all our differences, imagine all the lines of separation we as human beings have drawn between ourselves, our different beliefs, our different lifestyles, our different ways of thinking. Inhale all of it, slowly and deeply, into your chest. Hold everyone here in your heart. This is the formless space that we all share, the place of unconditional love. Imagine the lines of separation now beginning to fade away as you hold the whole world in your heart. Hold this for as long as it feels right to you. Your beautiful sacred heart chakra is beginning to glow a bright green.

Now, when you next exhale, do so out of the top of your head, and as you do, imagine rays of golden sunlight emitting out of your crown chakra. This is the mind of Christ. Old things are passing away, and all things are becoming new. Continue this meditation until the feeling of oneness fills your mind and body, this feeling generally coming around the 20-minute mark. This meditation's effects are potent and multiplied when practiced with a partner or in a group setting.

"This life's dim windows of the soul, distorts the heavens from pole to pole, and leads you to believe a lie, when you see with, not through the eye."

- William Blake

CHAPTER 5
CONSIDER THE LILIES

Negotiating reality requires faith. The good news is that faith is a skill that can be learned, and the more you use it, the better you become at it. The Bible says that all of us have been given a measure of faith. *"For I say, through the grace given unto me, to every man that is among you, not to think of himself more highly than he ought to think; but to think soberly, according as God hath dealt to every man the measure of faith"* (Romans 12:3).

This is more good news: you already have it! Think of it as if you were planning to take a trip out of the country. You would make sure that you packed everything that you were going to need for your journey. You would take clothing, cosmetics, toiletries, shoes, socks, underwear, toothbrush, etc.—and your passport. Faith is like your passport; it is required to enter a foreign land. Imagine, before you took this particular human incarnation, your bags were packed, and you came here with everything you needed for the trip, including your passport (faith); you wouldn't be here now having this human experience if you didn't have it, as it was required for entry.

So, what exactly is faith? The Bible says, *"Now faith is the substance of things hoped for, the evidence of things not seen"* (Hebrews 11:1). Another version of the scripture reads as *"Faith is the realization of what is hoped for and evidence of things not seen. Because of it the ancients were well attested. By faith we understand that the universe was ordered by the word of God, so that what is visible came into being through the invisible"* (Hebrews 11:1-3 NABRE).

As we talked about in the previous chapter, we can see how reality is created by faith. *"In the beginning God created the heaven and the earth. And the earth was without form and void"* (Genesis 1:1-2). This passage shows us the nature of our reality and how it comes into being. There is a void. Science refers to this as the Quantum Field, and in this field all possibilities exist. This field is all around us since it is the invisible space that fills the entire universe, and everything that we perceive as reality comes out of this space. You can access this field with your imagination, since all possibilities exist in your limitless imagination, and faith causes these invisible things to become visible to your physical eyes. Unseen reality becomes seen reality. The unseen reality is actually more real than the seen reality because it is the very source of everything seen. In other words, it's real before you even see it.

Christian mystic Neville Goddard said that "faith is loyalty to your unseen reality." Pause for a moment here, and think about that. Let it really sink in before we go any further. It works like this: have a clear intention of what you want, see it in your imagination, and try your best to feel the reality of it. Doing this lets you latch onto it in the quantum field with the lasso of faith. As you stay loyal to your imaginative act, you are pulling it toward you, and it will eventually manifest in your physical reality.

You may be tempted to say, "Yeah, sounds great and all, but it's easier said than done" or "I totally get it; however, it is simply not true." You have been given a measure of faith for the sole purpose of creating and negotiating reality. Now you just need to use it. Faith is already part of your makeup, and the more you use it, the better you will get at it; and the better you get at it, the better you are going to feel, and the better you feel, the easier it becomes for your desired unseen reality to manifest in your life.

I need to ask you something, and it's kind of a personal question, so bear with me here. Is your life pleasing to you? There is no right or wrong answer, complete honesty is the only thing required. One more time, is your current life pleasing to you? Maybe you answered yes, and maybe you answered no. Perhaps you even answered yes *and* no. Maybe some aspects of your reality are pleasing to you, others not so much. No worries either way, this can be easily fixed.

Scripture tells us that *"without faith, it is impossible to please God..."* (Hebrews 11:6 NIV). What does this mean? Well, you are God, so we could say, "Without faith, it is impossible to please yourself." If our current reality is not all that pleasing to us, it simply means we are not correctly using our measure of faith. That's really all that there is to it.

It's almost as if we came here to have this human experience and on our way through the dimensional portal we grabbed a toolkit and passed through the veil of forgetfulness. As a result of this, we ended up with our toolkit in hand and no earthly idea about how to use it. Some of us don't even know what the tools are let alone what they're for. If this is the case with you, it's all good. You can rest assured that it's not your fault, that's just the way it is.

One of the main power tools in your kit is faith. So, how do we use it? Once again, scripture serves as our user manual here. We read in Mark 11:23), *"For verily I say unto you, that whosoever will say unto this mountain, be thou removed, and be thou cast into the sea; and shall not doubt in his heart but shall believe that those things which he saith shall come to pass; he shall have whatsoever he saith."* If we look at the very next verse, we read, *"Therefore I say unto you, what things soever you desire, when ye pray, believe that ye receive them, and ye shall have them"* (Mark 11:24).

Faith is both extremely simple, and yet difficult at the same time. Simple in the fact that all we have to do is believe. Sounds easy, right? The difficult part is the business of not doubting. It's hard to believe something that you can't see with your physical eyes.

"Blessed are they who have not seen, and yet have believed" (John 20:29). This is what negotiating reality is all about. We have to believe before we see, and then we get to see. Seems kind of backward, doesn't it? It's pretty much the opposite of what our senses have taught us. With its army of minions (doubts), the ego is always ready to offer us its best advice: "Yeah, right, I'll believe it when I see it."

This is where many people get tripped up and often give up because they can't figure out how to avoid the onslaught of doubts that flood their minds whenever they are trying to have faith. Sound familiar?

You cannot have faith and avoid doubts at the same time. Read that again. You cannot have faith and avoid doubts at the same time. The key to faith is realizing that you simply cannot avoid doubts (noun). You can, however, avoid doubting (verb), and you do that by recognizing that doubts do not belong to you; they are not in you, and they are not yours. There is a world of difference between doubts and doubting. Doubts are snarky little things, and they don't want you to know they are separate from you because they do not want to be exposed.

Expose them! Don't try to avoid them because that will never work out in your favor. The strategy here is to acknowledge them, almost like cars passing by you on the highway. You don't go through life ultimately trying to avoid cars; otherwise, you would find it difficult to go anywhere.

Understanding that doubts exist outside of yourself, that they are not part of who you are, is a truth that will set you free! When you are creating and negotiating your reality, remaining loyal to your imaginative acts, and doubts creep into your awareness, simply acknowledge them. Wave at them if you want, or flip them off if you wish, and they will pass on by like an angry driver with road rage on the interstate. Don't engage with them, don't try and nudge them with your car—that can cause a wreck! Just witness them. You can say to yourself, "Oh look, there's doubt." By simply acknowledging doubts, you expose them, and when you expose them, they dissipate. They are only kept alive by your sustained attention to them, so just acknowledge them, and let 'em go!

This is how we *"walk by faith, not by sight"* (2 Cor. 5:7) and why we can *"call those things which are not, as though they were"* (Romans 4:17). We're told that this is what Abraham did all the time and it was accounted to him for righteousness. Righteousness simply means right thinking, that's all it means, and right thinking creates a more pleasing reality for us. As a person thinks, so are they. We maintain right thinking by acknowledging and exposing doubts. Don't give them your energy by focusing on them. Nothing more than a simple acknowledgment is needed. This is a powerful method for maintaining balance and negotiating reality.

Doubts are created when our external circumstances don't line up with what we believe. This is the contrast. But remember, faith is a skill you can strengthen, and the paradox is that faith can only be strengthened by contrast. When contrast appears, see it for what it is: an opportunity to strengthen your faith. This is why we read, *"Consider it pure joy, my brothers and sisters, whenever you face trials of many kinds, because you know that the testing of your faith produces perseverance. Let perseverance finish its work so that you may be mature and complete, not lacking anything"* (James 1:2-4 NIV).

The above verse is speaking of contrast, and we are told that when the contrast appears, to consider it pure joy because it is an opportunity to strengthen our faith. This is even more good news! Even the contrast is working for our higher good! All we have to do is trust the process of faith. It's a win-win: our faith is strengthened, and we won't be lacking anything.

If we accept this truth, and trust this process, then the waiting period between our imagined creations and their manifestation becomes like "short-timing" at a job. You know that feeling, we've all been there. You've been working at a terrible job for a while, and you've been wanting to quit, and you finally get the courage to put in your two weeks' notice. Suddenly, the next two weeks don't seem so bad because you're relieved. You know that it will all be over soon, and something new is going to begin. You might even enjoy your last few days there.

This waiting period between our imagined creations and their manifestation is known in scripture as the Sabbath. We are instructed to *"keep the sabbath"* (Exodus 31:16). We keep the Sabbath by letting doubts pass us by and not entertaining them. If we keep the Sabbath, God keeps the covenant. The covenant is: Our imagination creates reality. And because we and God are the same, reality is negotiable.

"And Jesus said unto him, no man, having put his hand to the plough, and looking back, is fit for the kingdom of God" (Luke 9:62). This passage is about the covenant and the Sabbath. Jesus is your wonderful human imagination. The plough is your imagined creation, the kingdom of God is your reality.

We are told here that there can be no looking back (entertaining doubts) if we want our creation to manifest, and we see this principle all throughout scripture. The story of Lot's wife (Genesis 19:26) is another great example. When she looks back and doubts her decision to leave her city, she is turned into a pillar of salt. In other words, her imagined creations just disintegrated and never manifested. Once you create your desire in your imagination, you must not start doubting, and you must leave your old ways of thinking behind if you want to see the manifestation in your physical reality.

Sometimes "not looking back" can be a bit slippery. Past experiences can be very stressful, and it can be very tempting to slide back into old thought patterns. Remember, you are not your past! *"Therefore, if any man be in Christ (imagination), he is a new creature: Old things have passed away; behold, all things have become new"* (2 Cor. 5:17).

The past has passed away. You are the only one who can raise it from the dead by reliving it in your mind, and you really don't want to do that, no matter how tempting it may seem. This is what the Apostle Paul was speaking of when he said, *"...I focus on this one thing: Forgetting the past and looking forward to what lies ahead"* (Phil. 3:13 NLT).

This is the golden rule of negotiating reality right here, in the present moment, and if you do nothing else in this book other than this, you would be ahead of the game. It is vital that you learn to forget the things that are behind. Where your attention goes, your energy flows. You definitely do not need your energy flowing into the dead past.

Look at it in terms of a relationship. You are in a loving marriage with Jesus Christ (your wonderful human imagination), don't be a cheater, don't have an affair with doubts. Remain loyal to your creative imagination, and together you will bring forth your beautiful creation.

While you wait for the due date, simply keep joyful anticipation going as much as possible. There's no need to panic or be anxious. You can go ahead and start preparing for the arrival if you wish.

Have fun with it! Have faith like a child. A child's chief aim is to have fun! You don't need to fret and worry about how your creation will arrive. You don't need to know exactly how everything is going to work out. The universe likes surprises, so let it surprise you!

We all like surprises, and we all like surprising other people with good things and good news. It's just something that's built into us, and it's based in love. There's nothing better than surprising someone you love with something they've been wanting. That moment is filled with pure joy. It makes you happy, and it makes them happy. We are in a loving relationship with the universe, and the inner workings of how your manifestation will come to be is the universe's surprise party for you. So don't spoil it by trying to figure it all out. Don't ruin the surprise!

It's like when a baby is about to be born. You don't know every little thing that is going on in the womb, and it's dark in there, but the baby is going to be born anyway. It works the same way, as you don't need to try and micromanage your manifestations. You just need to be there for the delivery. This is your act of faith. As above, so below.

The gospel of Matthew gives us a great example of what it's like to have faith. The word "gospel" means good news, and this is some good news right here: *"And Jesus called a little child unto him, and sat him in the midst of them, and said, verily I say unto you, except ye be converted, and become like little children, ye shall not enter the kingdom of heaven. Whosoever, therefore, shall humble himself as this little child, the same is greatest in the kingdom of heaven"* (Matthew 18:2-4).

So, what exactly is this scripture telling us? Let's unpack this and see how this applies to faith.

For starters, children love using their imaginations because it comes naturally to them, and they're very good at it. Now granted, they're not intentionally using their imaginations to negotiate reality at a young age, but they are using it to have fun, and this is very important for us as adults to understand. We should be enjoying life, and having fun using our imaginations! This is having faith like a child.

Another aspect of childlike faith, the main point of the above scripture, is that little children generally don't doubt, question, or seek explanations when promised something. In short, they trust.

"Whereby are given unto us exceeding great and precious promises: that by these ye might be partakers of the divine nature" (2 Peter 1:4). If we can simply trust in the promises of God, then we will be partakers of our own divine nature, and we can create a better world for ourselves and others. We are instructed to trust God, which is you, which is me, which is we. You need to have faith and trust in your own divine nature. In other words, bet on you! Do not doubt yourself—and most of all, don't worry about how things are going to work out. Just trust that they will. Worry cannot solve anything; it only robs you of your peace in the present moment.

"That is why I tell you not to worry about your everyday life, whether you have enough food and drink, or enough clothes to wear. Isn't life more than food, and your body more than clothing? Look at the birds. They don't plant or harvest or store food in barns, for your heavenly Father feeds them. And aren't you far more valuable to him than they are? Can all your worries add a single moment to your life? And why worry about your clothing? Look at the lilies of the field and how they grow. They don't work or make their clothing, yet Solomon in all his glory was not dressed as beautiful as they are. And if God cares so wonderfully for wildflowers that are here today and thrown into the fire tomorrow, he will certainly care for you. Why do you have so little faith? So don't worry about these things, saying, 'What shall we eat? What shall we drink? What will we wear?' These things dominate the thoughts of unbelievers, but your heavenly Father already knows all your needs. Seek the kingdom of God above all else, and live righteously, and he will give you everything you need. So don't worry about tomorrow, for tomorrow will bring its own worries. Today's trouble is enough for today" (Matthew 6:25-34 NLT).

If we read the above passage of scripture carefully, with the eyes of the spirit, or as "new wine," we will see that Jesus is pointing to something greater than what we can perceive with our physical senses. The Bible's message is often hidden behind the mere words printed on the page.

Jesus begins this verse by telling us not to worry about our everyday life, and then he asks a question: Isn't life more than food and the body more than clothing? Food and clothing represent our outer world, and he is saying that there's something more than this. He then gives an example of the birds and how they don't work or store food in barns because their supply is coming from another source apart from their physical reality. This "Source" is referred to as Heavenly Father (the unseen and formless universal consciousness that provides for all creation). We are told not to worry about our daily lives because we are highly valued by this Source, and worrying won't add anything to our lives; we only take away from it.

This Source is us, the loving awareness behind all of our outer forms. Jesus is telling us here that we shouldn't just be focusing on our outer circumstances. He's not suggesting this because they don't matter, but because there is something so much bigger at work here, and when we are only concerned with the cares of daily life, our nose to the grindstone, it causes us to lose touch with the Source within us. This causes worry, panic, and fearful thoughts, which do not serve us in any way.

We are asked to trust and believe in this loving Source which provides for us daily, and to not let our minds be dominated with thoughts of lack and unbelief in ourselves. Our divine nature already knows everything that we need, and if we take our attention off our outer world and place it on our inner world, we will see that all things are possible with God. This is faith. If we seek the kingdom of God first (our loving, all-providing divine nature), everything will work out for our ultimate good.

EXERCISE OF FAITH
Duration: 10-20 minutes

This exercise is most effective right before bed. Lie down on your back, close your eyes and take several slow, deep breaths and relax to the fullest as you prepare for sleep.

Begin to replay the events of the day in your mind, starting with the last thing and working your way back to the start of your day. Walk through each event in your mind, acknowledging everything you did throughout the day. When you are back at the start, let it all go.

Lie there in the darkness, bringing your attention inward, and realize now that you are the awareness that just observed everything you did today. Rest in this awareness and feel the cares of daily life drift away as you drift closer to sleep. Feel the loving, warm presence of your divine nature permeating your physical body. This is real, this is you. You are resting in the presence of the divine Source where all possibilities exist.

Here, in this place, trusting in this presence, begin to see your life as you would like it to be and know that it has your best interest at heart. Feel the relief of knowing that you no longer need to worry about your life. Fall asleep in this feeling.

"To see a world in a grain of sand and a heaven in a wildflower, hold infinity in the palm of your hand, and eternity in an hour."

- William Blake

CHAPTER 6

REVISION

In the previous chapter, we discussed the importance of forgetting those things that we have already left behind. We were also reminded that the divine Source always has our best interests at heart because the Source is God, and God is us, and we are the Source. In this chapter, we will take this understanding one step further.

I want to share with you one of Neville Goddard's most sacred techniques that proves reality is, in fact, negotiable. I encourage you—no, I dare you—to experiment with these techniques and prove to yourself the neuroplastic nature of reality.

Neville referred to this reality creation technique as "Revision," which, at its core, is the ultimate practice of forgiveness. The only prerequisite is your willingness to dispel your current understanding and belief about time. Time is a fabricated concept. There is really no such thing, and science is now proving that what we refer to as "time" does not travel along a linear path. There is only the present moment, and what you do in this moment affects every aspect of your reality—past, present, and future.

Imagine you are standing on the bank of a peaceful, quiet pond, and you pick up a small stone and throw it into the middle of the water. What happens? It would make a splash, and then you would see the ripples going out in circles in all directions all at once—forward, backward, left, and right. This can be difficult to wrap our heads around, but this is how the present moment works. Everything is happening everywhere all at once.

"He has made everything beautiful in its time. He has also set eternity in the human heart..." (Ecclesiastes 3:11 NIV). In the Bible, the word "heart" is interchangeable with the word "mind," and the word "eternity" means all of time, past, present, and future. So, we could read this as "He has made everything beautiful in its time. He has also put the past, present and the future into the mind of man." You are the I AM, you are God, and all of eternity exists in your mind. The whole vast universe is mental, and no matter where you perceive yourself in time, you are only, and always, and for eternity, in the present moment.

We are in the eternal present moment, and understanding that past, present, and future exist right here means that what we do now can and does affect the past, which affects our present, which affects our future. It may be a good idea to pause and quietly ponder that for a few moments before going further.

We all have things in our past that we're not proud of, things that happened years ago that still tend to haunt us to this day. Many people today are struggling with the repercussions from events that happened in their past. Some of us (like my wife) lived through an extremely traumatic childhood, while some of us had what the world would consider a "normal" childhood, with a few negative events here and there. An important thing to remember is our sense of "oneness." We all come from various backgrounds with different experiences, but also, we are all connected. We are all in this together.

When it comes to revision, the various degrees of severity of past negative events are a nonissue. This very powerful method of negotiating reality can reach into childhood, adulthood, the deep past or the recent past, and all moments of our human life experience. The definition of revision is "to re-examine and make alterations. To reconsider and amend, especially in the light of further evidence or to reflect a changed situation."

In essence, revision is going back and changing past events from something undesirable to something desirable. From something unpleasant to pleasant. From something that haunts us to something that blesses us. Neville Goddard often suggested that the act of revision was the most powerful and life-changing thing one could do for oneself. He encouraged everyone to do this throughout their lives, even recommending doing this daily every night before falling asleep by revising the day.

It's actually very simple, and I believe this is why it's not that commonly practiced or talked about outside of new thought circles. *"But God hath chosen the foolish (simple) things of the world to confound the wise..."* (1 Cor. 1:27). I believe that if the technique of revision were to be practiced by the masses daily, the world could change in the blink of an eye.

The idea of revision is not a foreign concept, for clinical psychologists all over the world know full well the dramatic effects that revision can have on people who have a troubled past. Past Regression Therapy is very similar in many ways to Neville's technique. Past Regression Therapy consists of going back into our past via hypnosis and uncovering an unwanted event that, due to its severity, caused us to bury it deep in our subconscious mind. In this intensive and emotional process, we rediscover this event and realize and understand that this is the source of our current life issues, and then the long journey of healing from that event begins.

Revision, by contrast, is the process of rewriting the past using our creative imaginations in such a way that it projects into our present. Neuroscientific research shows that neurons in the brain that fire together also wire together. This means that as you revise a past event in your mind, if you can feel its emotion as if it were a present reality, the neurons begin to fire together and wire themselves together to form a new memory of the event. I am not a scientist by any means, but I have found that a general understanding of what's happening inside our brains adds validity to the revision technique.

I think it's safe to say that Neville was significantly ahead of his time by being in the eternal present moment. Long before any current research was available, he discovered the miracle-working power of revision. He made it his life goal to share his findings with as many people as possible. It all hinges, however, on the assumption of us knowing that we are God. We are omnipotent, we are omnipresent, and we are omniscient; as a result, revision is available to us as an ever-present technique for negotiating reality.

Let me also say that the revision technique is not a "one and done" feat. This is a process. We are the authors and the finishers of our life stories, but we should not assume that by waving the magic wand of revision over our past that suddenly everything is going to come up wine and roses. However, with consistent practice of this technique, we will begin to see the results we desire.

Revision can be used at any time, and we can use it for something major or something incidental. I recommend starting small and then gradually working your way into larger revisions. If, at the end of the day today, as you reflect on the events that happened earlier in the morning or afternoon and things didn't go as planned, this is a great starting point to get your feet wet with revision. Perhaps you had an unpleasant conversation with a co-worker, and it's bothering you; maybe you got angry at your kids, or you received an unnerving phone call from your ex, making your blood boil. These are all perfect candidates for revision.

When you think about the events of your day, use your imagination to rewrite the script. How would you have preferred things had gone? What would have been the more desirable outcome? Take your time with this, and as you see the revised event playing out in your mind, you will eventually feel a sense of relief flood your body, a peace that surpasses all understanding. If at first you are not feeling a sense of relief, not to worry; this is normal. You simply have not felt the reality of it just yet, but you will. Replay the revised scene again, and each time you do, focus on the feeling you would expect to have if the unwanted event had gone the way you desired. This takes some practice and getting used to, but once you feel the sensation of relief, then the event has been successfully revised.

I would like to share my wife's personal experience with revision because I believe it will help bolster your faith in your abilities to use this technique.

My wife had a painful childhood, so much so that she lived much of her young adult life in a perpetual state of fight or flight. When she first learned about revision, she began to test the technique with small events in her recent past, such as an argument with a family member that happened a few days earlier. She revised that event, and in her imagination, she experienced the conversation as being pleasant, with no argument whatsoever. She practiced this a few times, felt the relief, and believed it had been revised. A day later, she received a phone call from the same family member, and it was as if the argument had never happened. They had a lovely conversation, and all was well.

This experience caused her to believe that revision works, but she was still uncertain that she was capable of revising something big from her distant past. However, she was determined to give it a try, and that's all Neville ever asked anyone to do, simply to try. You can never fully believe in something that you have not personally experienced. Try it for yourself...just try.

One day, upon returning home from work, I found my wife crying alone in the bathroom. I was immediately concerned by this and began to console her, putting my arm around her and asking her what was wrong.

"Nothing is wrong," she said in a trembling voice, tears streaming down her face.

"Then why are you crying and shaking? What happened?" I asked.

"It worked, oh my God, Justin, it worked!" she said, wiping the tears from her cheeks.

"What worked?" I asked curiously.

"Revision. It really worked!" she insisted.

I later found out that while I was at work, she had been using the revision technique to amend a very emotional and disturbing event from her childhood that she should never have witnessed and has carried with her ever since. The event was violent and involved numerous family members, along with her grandmother, whom she loved dearly.

As she was revising the past event, her grandmother appeared to her in her imagination in perfect form, a younger healthier version of herself, and she gave my wife a hug and said, "Thank you so much for taking the time to do this, I love you." A sense of relief washed over my wife at that moment, and she knew beyond a shadow of a doubt that the event had been successfully revised. Somehow, outside of our understanding of space and time, this one event was changed for the better. You never really know what you're capable of until you try. Why not pick up a stone and throw it into the middle of the pond?

REVISION EXERCISE FOR BEGINNERS
Duration: Varies

Think of a small unwanted event in your recent past, no more than a few days ago, if possible, so that it's still fresh on your mind. This can be anything from just a general annoyance, bad customer service, someone taking your parking spot, being stuck in traffic, you were late to work, and so forth. Any small thing that you wish had gone differently.

This next step is optional, but I find it very beneficial: Grab a piece of paper and write down the revised version of the event as you would have liked it to have happened. Script it. Read it over a few times as if you're an actor memorizing your lines. Now go into your imagination and visualize the event playing out as you wrote it. You can replay the event in your mind as many times as needed, and when you feel the sense of relief and satisfaction that it is now as you desire it to be, when it feels natural, then release it.

Congratulate yourself on a job well done!

Experiment with this technique, have fun with it, and know that you will become more efficient as you go along. Revision is a wonderful tool that can be a very helpful companion along our spiritual path; however, if it doesn't feel natural or right for you, that's okay, too. No worries, you do what feels best for you.

"I sought my God and my God I could not find; I sought my soul, and my soul eluded me. I sought to serve my brother in his need, and found all three; my God, my soul, and thee."

- William Blake

CHAPTER 7

BECOME FAMILIAR

Growing up in church and later working in full-time Christian ministry, the general assumption was that believers "prayed" and the heathen "meditated." Meditation was looked upon as something sinful, something that you shouldn't tamper with lest you become corrupted by Satan. I'm not kidding, that's what we were taught to believe. Meditation was something that only "New-Agers" engaged in, and it made them crazy in the head. It is almost as if some organized religion's chief aim is to keep us as far away from our true selves as possible so that we never find out that we are God—because, at that point, the jig is up!

It's funny, though, because the word meditation simply means "to become familiar with." Some churches don't want people to meditate and become familiar with themselves because, to them, the self is something to be controlled and disciplined. Let me be clear: I'm not saying that all churches are like this, but I also know that I am not alone in my experience.

But I digress. Even the Bible speaks of meditation, not just once but numerous times, and it's referred to as something holy and desirable, a way of honoring God.

Prayer, in its original Hebrew sense, means "a form of contemplation," so it seems that meditation and prayer are essentially one and the same. Regardless of which term you prefer, it is, in fact, something that produces life-changing results in the lives of those who engage with it.

When it comes to negotiating reality, the more familiar we become with our true selves and the world in which we live, the more empowered we feel. When we feel empowered, we have the confidence to create a better reality for ourselves and those around us.

There are a myriad of books written about prayer and meditation, and this is a good thing. Yet with all that information floating around and all the various ideas and beliefs, it is important to know that there is no such thing as a bad meditation. There is no wrong way to pray. You do you. Never let a pastor, guru, teacher, author, or any friend or family member tell you otherwise. You are the I AM, and what feels right to you is right for you. Simply experiment with prayer and meditation in all its various forms, and practice the one that yields the greatest results in your life.

In my life, the turning point came when I changed my viewpoint of Jesus. I stopped looking at him and started looking through him. A major shift in reality occurs when you no longer see him as something separate and outside of yourself. He never was, and never will be, anything other than you. When you no longer regard him as someone you pray to but pray through, you realize that you do not actually have a viewpoint of God, but rather, you are the viewpoint of God.

If you would like a scriptural reference for this, you will find it in 2 Cor.

5:16. *"Wherefore henceforth know we no man after the flesh: yea, though we have known Christ after the flesh, yet now henceforth know we him no more."* The Apostle Paul is telling us that we, himself included, used to view Christ as a physical human being who walked the earth, but not anymore. There is a big difference between the writings of Paul and other New Testament writers. Read his writings carefully, and you will understand that his main theme is that we can, and will be, transformed by the renewing of our minds when we see God as our consciousness (both personal and universal) rather than as a separate entity outside of ourselves.

There is another esoteric reference to this found in Luke 24:28-31: *"And they drew nigh unto the village, whither they went: and he made as though he would have gone further. But they constrained him, saying, abide with us: for it is toward evening, and the day is far spent. And he went in to tarry with them. And it came to pass, as he sat at meat with them, he took bread, and blessed it, and brake, and gave to them. And their eyes were opened, and they knew him; and he vanished out of their sight."*

The Bible is a book of psychological symbols. It is a message to the soul and must be psychologically interpreted to discover its true meaning. The above passage is a symbolic reference that shows that when our eyes are truly opened, we will see Jesus as our own human imagination. The physical conception of him we used to have will vanish. I encourage you to read the rest of that story, as it shows us the magnificent difference between knowing about Jesus Christ and actually *knowing* Jesus Christ. Many of us know about him. Pretty much the whole world knows about him, but if we see him as anything other than our own wonderful human imagination, we don't really know him.

This is where Neville Goddard was coming from when he referred to the entire universe as nothing more than ourselves pushed out. Everyone and everything is you. It's all imagination, so we regard no one as according to the flesh.

Can you see where the disconnect arises in prayer? If everything is mental, and yet we are praying to someone whom we perceive as outside that construct, then there is literally no way in the world that this can achieve anything. It's praying to someone or something that quite literally doesn't exist.

We are all unique and individualized viewpoints of the One. Your life is significant because the way God experiences life through you is something only you can provide. It's a unique part of the story of life that belongs to you and only you.

Life itself is happening through you!

Jesus gives us a glimpse beyond the veil of what prayer and meditation are in Matthew 6:6: *"But thou, when thou prayest, enter into thy inner room, and when thou hast shut the door, pray to your father which is in secret; and thy father which seeth in secret shall reward thee openly."* Reality negotiation 101 right here! We enter into our inner room (our imagination) and we shut the door (close out all sensory distractions, negative thoughts, the cares of the world). In this state we create what we desire in our mind, in secret, not telling anyone what we're up to. Our Father (consciousness) hears us, and our creations then manifest openly in our physical reality.

This is prayer.

The reason why personal prayer should be done in secret, is because the human ego will start the wheels of doubt spinning if it is done openly—that's just how it is. If you tell people what you're up to, generally they will respond, "Oh okay, sure, sounds good, but just how is that supposed to happen?" And when you're praying for someone else, such as for healing, well-being, prosperity, love, the same thing can happen: they may begin to question whether the prayer will be answered or not. Just keep it secret, and when it manifests, you'll have the satisfaction of knowing exactly what you did for them. Life likes surprises, remember?

The importance of prayer and meditation cannot be overstated, and it's definitely something that we should all be working into our daily schedule. I used to believe that prayer was asking God for things, and then when those things didn't happen, eventually prayer turned into begging, and then the begging turned into pleading. It was always centered around me, and if my prayers would continue to go unanswered, I would begin to question my faith and try to figure out what I was doing wrong. The TV preachers didn't help. They made it sound that if you have true faith in God, then you wouldn't get so much as a headache. I would wonder if I had some unconfessed sin in my life that was hindering my prayers or even if God was hearing me at all. It can go on and on, and it's a nasty rabbit hole to go down. Unfortunately, a lot of people spend their lives spiraling down there.

Don't get me wrong, I prayed all the time, for myself and for others, but it's hard to have confidence in something when the results are so rarely experienced. This is a universal issue. Everything changes; however, when you realize that you and God are one and the same, prayer simply becomes your creative act. You're no longer trying to twist the arm of some deity to act on your behalf but rather causing reality to react on your behalf. Our reality doesn't respond to what we want. It responds to who we are. There's a scripture that shows us how this universal law operates: *"For whosoever hath, to him shall be given, and he shall have more abundance: but whosoever hath not, from him shall be taken away even that he hath"*

(Matthew 13:12).

This verse is referring to those who know who they are and what they have. They know their divine nature and they know in consciousness that all things are possible. An abundant state of mind attracts abundance. In your "inner room," your mind, you know who you are. Regardless of your external circumstances, in your imagination you are the one "who has." If we can successfully make this our state of being (the state of having), then more will be given.

It's not always the easiest thing to do, trust me, I get it, but it really is all in the mind. Our reality is but a shadow cast from our inner state of being. Change happens from the inside out, and prayer and meditation are what bring about the changes we would like to see.

One of the aspects of reality creation that many would-be manifestors get tripped up on is the time buffer between our prayer and its manifestation in our physical world. We create in our imagination, some time goes by, we don't see it yet, and we lose faith. Instead, if we can learn to appreciate this gestation period and realize that it's here for our benefit, then it becomes an asset to us. It's just part of our 3D reality in this particular dimension of dense matter—things take time. Thank God! Can you imagine what would happen if everyone's imaginal acts manifested instantly? Our reality would be total chaos!

There are levels or planes of existence, such as the astral plane, a non-physical plane where thoughts immediately materialize. There are planes upon planes. I can't speak with any credibility about those other dimensions, but I do have some experience with the astral plane and can tell you that a timeline does not exist there. Perhaps you have experienced this yourself when the moment you think about something, it happens instantly. This can be startling if you're not accustomed to it. That's why you have to leave your physical body to go to the astral plane. Our astral body, or the energy body, can handle it since it has no problem negotiating that reality. Our physical bodies, on the other hand, not so much. We'll talk more about this fascinating aspect of reality negotiation soon, but for now, let's get back to prayer and meditation.

So, here in this current reality, where things move in time, we are forced to deal with the waiting period between our imaginative acts and their physical manifestations. It's just part of reality. Think of it like ordering something online. You order it (perform the act) and now you just have to wait for it to arrive. Sometimes there is next day free shipping, sometimes there's same day delivery, but oftentimes not. When I was young, we ordered things from catalogs, and let me tell you it often took six to eight weeks for it to arrive! Either way though, sooner or later, it arrives and it's all good. There's nothing to worry about. You have a tracking number, so you know it's on the way.

Belief (faith) is like your spiritual tracking number. It is the evidence of things not seen, remember? Jesus lays it out clearly in Mark 11:24: *"Therefore I say unto you, what things soever ye desire, when ye pray, believe that ye receive them, and ye shall have them."*

There are a couple of very important things we need to understand in this verse. First, the words "what things soever ye desire," can be anything. You can create anything. Consciousness does not judge good, bad, or indifferent. All things are possible. The second thing we need to understand, and this is the crux of it, to "believe that ye receive." Or, a more accurate way to say this would be, "believe that you have already received." Neville referred to this in many of his lectures as "living from the end." Praying in this manner, believing that you have already received the thing desired, puts you smack dab in the middle of being "one who has." If we pray from any other position, we are praying as "one who has not" and our reality reflects that back to us. Always remember: The universe is a mirror.

For some people, when they pray they can easily visualize what they desire. They can see things clearly and in great detail. For others, visualizing is more difficult. But what I have found is that those who struggle with visualizing often have a heightened sense of "feeling" the reality of their desires. This is true for me. It is easier for me to enter into a state of "feeling" my desire than it is to clearly see it. This is something that is often not clarified. Just because you're not a master visualizer does not mean you can't be a master manifester! Both feeling and visualizing are equally effective.

Try it, and do not get discouraged or frustrated because you have a hard time seeing a clear mental picture. Know that you'll get better with practice. Try to feel the reality of your wish fulfilled. For instance, if you're hoping to receive a raise at your job, go into your prayer or meditation and imagine what it would feel like to get that raise. How would you feel it in your body? How would you feel emotionally? Would you feel dizzy with happiness? Would you not be able to stop smiling? Imagine that it has already happened, and feel that feeling. Feel the appropriate emotion of it.

There's a great example of this found in Luke 8:42-48. "*...But as he went the people thronged him. And a woman having an issue of blood twelve years, which had spent all her living upon physicians, neither could be healed of any, came behind him, and touched the border of his garment: and immediately her issue of blood stanched. And Jesus said, who touched me? When all denied, Peter and they that were with him said, Master, the multitude throng thee and press thee, and sayest thou, Who touched me? And Jesus said, Somebody hath touched me: for I perceive (feel) that virtue is gone out* *of me. And when the woman saw that she was not hid, she came trembling, and falling down before him, she declared unto him before all the people for what cause she had touched him, and how she was healed immediately. And he said unto her, Daughter, be of good comfort: thy faith has made thee whole; go in peace."*

In the above verse, you are the woman, and you are Jesus. The woman touched Jesus (imagination) in faith (believing), and there was a "feeling" of virtue (emotion). Imagination mixed with the feeling of already receiving what you desire, is the magical elixir of miracles. The power is in the feeling.

I know you can do this because we are emotional creatures. Hold the idea of what you desire in your mind and feel the feeling of already having it. Your emotion is your "virtue." When you can feel an emotion in relation to the idea in your mind, then you've "touched Jesus," and you've got it! All you must do now is wait with a casual expectancy, and it will appear in your reality. It's like fishing. Cast your line with your imagination, hook the fish with the feeling, and know then you can confidently reel it in.

As mentioned earlier, meditation means "to become familiar with," and you can familiarize yourself with whatever you desire during meditation. Also, a good practice is to simply become familiar with yourself. I have found that white noise works very well for this type of meditation. With this method you are simply sitting quietly with yourself. Perhaps you have white noise playing through some headphones, and you just sit. Just be. You can do this for as long as you wish, but twenty minutes seems to be a good starting point. If you don't have headphones or access to white noise, anything can work—the hum of an air conditioner or a fan; anything that can occupy the auditory part of your mind for a little while will work just fine.

You'll be amazed at what you can learn about yourself during these sessions. I suggest you keep a notebook and pen handy so you can easily jot down whatever comes to mind.

There are innumerable different forms of meditation out there, and as mentioned earlier, there is no shortage of books on the topic, not to mention the thousands of YouTube videos available. I just wanted to mention the above meditation because it's a simple one that anybody can do immediately and is essential for getting familiar with our higher selves. It really packs a metaphysical punch when practiced on a regular basis! Consistency is key.

Another key part of prayer and meditation that is too often overlooked but vital to getting the results you desire is setting your intention before you begin. The power of intention cannot be overstated. Try to have a clear and heartfelt intention in mind before you enter into your prayer or meditation. What are you hoping to achieve during this sacred time? What desire is truly in your heart?

The idea here is to achieve heart-mind coherence. You accomplish this state of coherence by wrapping your mind around what's in your heart. In other words, your mind needs to be able to perceive your heart's desire as an attainable reality. When this happens, you have a direct line of energy that flows untethered into the field of infinite possibilities.
"...With God, all things are possible" (Matthew 19:26).

When there is no heart-mind coherence established due to lack of intention, we become what the Bible refers to as "double-minded." *"But let him pray in faith, nothing wavering. For he that wavereth is like a wave of the sea driven by the wind and tossed. For let not that man think he shall receive anything from the lord. A double minded man is unstable in all his ways"*

(James 1:6-8).

A lack of heart-mind coherence creates instability, and we don't want that! What we want is what Jesus describes in Mark 11:23. *"For verily I say unto you, that whosoever shall say unto this mountain, be thou removed and be thou cast into the sea; and shall believe in his heart and not doubt that those things which he saith shall come to pass, he shall have whatsoever he saith."*

Nothing is impossible—nothing in the whole vast world is impossible. If you can believe it in your heart and not doubt in your mind, then you become like an artist, and the world becomes a blank canvas waiting for you to enter the studio of your own wonderful, creative imagination.

One more aspect of prayer and meditation that often gets overlooked is the aspect of forgiveness. We read in Mark 11:25-27: *"...when you stand praying, forgive, if ye have aught against any: That your father also which is in Heaven may forgive you your trespasses. But if you do not forgive, neither will your father, which is in Heaven, forgive your trespasses."*

Most people do not associate forgiveness with meditation, but it's important that we understand the relationship between the two. We are all one. We are all fragments of the Source, and everyone in the entire world is simply ourselves pushed out. Understanding this, if we have an issue with someone, we really only have an issue with ourselves. We need to resolve these issues with mental forgiveness before we enter into prayer and meditation so that our energy is not stifled, which frees us up to create with our unlimited potential.

Where our attention goes, our energy flows. Through the act of mental forgiveness toward another, we take our attention off the "issue," and thus, we no longer waste our energy in that direction. Someone once said that harboring unforgiveness is like drinking poison and expecting the other person to die. If you have a chance to extend forgiveness towards someone in your physical reality face to face, by all means, do it. If that is not possible or desired, the act of forgiving them in your heart and mind will free you, causing symbiosis to occur, where forgiveness is extended toward you as well. It's a win-win!

Also, do not neglect to forgive yourself. (The revision method works well for this.) A lot of people have some sort of negative self-talk that tends to run on an endless loop in their heads. This stems from them never forgiving themselves. This negative dialogue can often keep one from receiving their desire because deep inside, they believe they are not worthy to receive it. Nothing could be further from the truth. We can be our own worst enemy sometimes, but we can also be our greatest asset. Forgive yourself and get on your own team! For many people, the act of self-forgiveness can create heart-mind coherence.

The Bible tells us to *"Pray without ceasing"* (1 Thes. 5:17). Well, that sounds great, but how is that even possible? It's only possible with the use of our imagination. Thoughts become reality. You often hear people say things like, "You're in our thoughts" or "Our prayers are with you." Now, it stands to reason that when people say things like this, it's normally just a formality without any real intention behind it; however, it really takes no effort at all to put a little "oomph" behind those words with the immense power of imagination.

For instance, say you're driving to work and you see a homeless person standing on the side of the road, and they're holding a sign that reads: "Will work for food." If you have the means to give them some money or to offer them employment, that's wonderful, and if you feel so compelled, you should do that. Yet it only takes a moment to see them in a better situation in your imagination. When you're sitting there at the stoplight, imagine them receiving the assistance they need, or imagine them gainfully employed in your mind's eye. Imagine them off the street, perhaps sitting around the dinner table with their family, smiling, laughing, and enjoying themselves. As long as it's something that you would like for yourself, imagine it for them. Thoughts become reality, and this is a wonderful habit to develop as it strengthens the muscles of your wonderful imagination.

It's not feasible to think that we could physically help everyone in need that crosses our daily path. We help them when we are able, of course, but we can always create something better for them in our imagination, which is the true source of creation.

A cool thing about this is that due to the law of reciprocity and because we are all one, as we do unto others, it is done unto us. This verse says that the righteous (those who practice this right way of thinking) will go through life with eternal joy, and those who refuse to think the best for others will go through life self-punished by their lack of imaginal generosity. "What goes around, comes around." This is a common thread that runs through all the world's major religions. It's not that some external God is punishing anybody, but their refusal to think the best for others simply reflects back on them from the mirror of life.

As you do this, you will find it amazingly fulfilling. When you form a habit of thinking wonderful thoughts for other people all the time, then you suddenly become aware that you have been "praying without ceasing."

For starters, it's a great way to eliminate boredom. It's also a great way to practice your imaginative and visualization skills. Practice makes perfect. It also engages you with the Golden Rule: Do unto others as you would have them do unto you. Can you see how this works? You are thinking and imagining great things for others all day long, and others are thinking and imagining great things for you all day in return. We're all in this together. Life is meant to be enjoyable, and this is one easy thing that we can do that makes a huge impact on our day-to-day reality. It's mutually beneficial for everyone involved.

Another advanced and more intimate technique can be used when we pray for others. We spoke earlier about assuming the identity and character traits of the ideal version of yourself and thereby becoming it. This same method can be utilized in praying for others with whom we have a more intimate relationship, such as close family members, friends, and co-workers.

Neville Goddard spoke of this technique in only one of his hundreds of lectures that I am aware of. The idea is that you can actually assume the identity of the person you are praying for during your prayer or meditation. You feel what it feels like to be them with as much detail as possible and bring in all the tones of reality to the best of your ability.

If the person you are praying for is in poor health and you wish them to be healthy and whole, imagine their improved state of being in as much detail as possible. Try to feel what it feels like to be them, and then feel health and vitality coursing through their physical body.

I used this method when my adopted brother was in the hospital with a serious condition. The doctors had given him only five days to live. I assumed his state of being. I felt myself to be him and visualized him walking around the hospital room, packing up his stuff because he was being released. Five days later, he didn't die as everyone expected. He was discharged and returned home. I told no one what I had done. I didn't even tell my brother I was praying for him. Everyone assumed it was a miracle. *"And the prayer of faith shall save the sick, and the Lord shall raise him up; and if he have committed sins, they shall be forgiven him"* (James 5:15).

If you are praying for someone who is experiencing financial difficulties, assume their state of being and feel the feeling of financial security on their behalf. Feel the feeling of relief that would be theirs if the financial difficulty had disappeared.

This method of prayer fulfills the scripture that says, *"Bear ye one another's burdens, and so fulfill the law of Christ"* (Galatians 6:2). When we pray in this manner, we operate within the law of Christ (imagination), which guarantees the result we desire, for every desire contains within itself everything necessary for its fulfillment.

SELF-MEDITATION EXERCISE
Duration: 10–20 Minutes

Set a clear intention in your mind. If possible, listen to white noise while doing this meditation. Find a comfortable place to sit with your spine straight. Have a pen and notebook ready at your side. Take seven deep relaxing breaths, inhaling through the nose and exhaling out the mouth. Feel your body relaxing deeper with each breath.

Sit quietly and simply observe your thoughts that will be random and all over the place at first, which is normal. The randomness will eventually dissipate as you relax and go deeper within. It is in this deep place within yourself where your creative ideas live. As they rise to the surface of your consciousness, write them down. Continue this meditation as long as it feels right for you.

Believe that you have received your intention during this time because you have in fact received it. If you don't realize it at first, that's fine; it will come to you throughout the day or night. Believe that you have already received it, and you shall have it.

IMMERSIVE PRAYER EXERCISE
Duration: 10–20 Minutes

Assume the identity of someone close to you for whom you would like to pray. Try to really feel what it feels like to be them. For instance, if they have long hair, imagine the hair draped over your shoulders as if it were yours. Literally put yourself into their state of being. You are merging with them during this practice. What does their body type feel like? Mentally immerse yourself in their identity, in their reality, in their skin.

Now, pray and or meditate as you would for yourself. You are feeling them into a desired state of being. When it feels real and a general sense of relief comes over you, then that's your cue that it's done. Tell no one about this, and when you see the desired results out in the open, you will be in absolute awe of the power you possess.

"Those who restrain desire do so because theirs is weak enough to be restrained."

- William Blake

CHAPTER 8

CONTENT CREATOR

The whole vast world is full of states.

For instance, if you look at a map of the United States of America, you will see all the different states that make up this country. These states collectively make up the whole of the United States. You are free to get into your car, or on a bus, a train or a plane and travel to any one of those states that you choose. You are also free to visit that state for as long as you wish. You can even move there and take up permanent residence.

All the various states have different qualities about them, some cold harsh climates, and some warm tropical climates. Some have mountains, others have oceans and sandy beaches, while others are flat and full of endless prairie. The landscape and terrain change as you travel across the country. Each state also has laws under which they operate, some of the laws are the same as in other states, and some are unique to that particular state.

The universe is physical, but it is also mental, and just like the physical reality in which we are having this human experience, the mental aspect of the universe is also full of various states. In fact, an easy way to see this principle of multiple realities is to realize that right now you are existing in at least two states. While you are in a mental state of mind, you are also in a geographical, physical state.

Every one of us passes through various states during our human incarnation on this planet. These are states of mind, and if a particular state of mind is persisted in, then it begins to concretize and become a state of being.

We all experience this, and we are currently experiencing it right now—it's how life operates. Currently, you are in a state. Take a moment to become aware of the current state you are in. This is a good practice to adopt, simply acknowledging your state of mind throughout the day. When you notice a shift in your mood, take a moment and become aware that you are entering into another state of mind. This simple practice gives you the upper hand as the observer of your reality—not just a participant (or a victim).

People who go through their daily lives unaware that they are passing through various states of mind may be easily affected by their circumstances and their immediate environment. The goal is to put a stop to this and realize that we are free to enter any state of our choosing. We are not forced by anyone or anything to enter a state against our will. When we don't realize that we are free to enter different states, then we also don't realize that we can leave a state at any time.

This type of unconscious living creates imbalance, and imbalance is not ideal for negotiating reality. We become like a wave of the sea, tossed to and fro by the winds of circumstance. We want balance, but balance is established when we are grounded in our state of being. Ask yourself right now what your current state of being is. A state of being is different from a state of mind: it is our normal everyday vibe. Are you an optimist? Are you a pessimist? Is the glass half full all the time, or is it always half empty? There is no right or wrong answer. Self-honesty is all that is required.

As mentioned earlier, a state of mind that is persisted in will eventually become our state of being. Sometimes, an unfortunate phenomenon occurs: a person's state of being is a whirlwind of various states of mind. This happens when a person is unaware that they are constantly passing through various states of mind, and their state of being becomes indecisive. They think that this is what reality is, and for them, it is very real. They struggle to make decisions and will argue with themselves for hours about something as simple as what to eat for dinner.

I'm sure you have experienced this. You and your spouse or a friend are going to go out to eat, and the struggle begins. "Where do you want to go?" "Well, we could go here, but..." "Or we could go there..." On and on it goes, until it's just easier to make a peanut butter and jelly sandwich rather than have a nice dinner out on the town. This situation is caused by not grounding in a pleasant state of being. These types of people generally benefit from someone else telling them where to go and what to do—and that's okay, but it's not ideal for someone who wants to negotiate their reality.

As far as states of being go, there is only one that produces stability in every aspect of our lives: contentment. We need to turn to our spiritual buddy, the Apostle Paul (who himself is a state, as are all characters in the Bible), to see what this state of contentment entails and how we can make it our state of being.

"Not that I speak in respect of want: for I have learned in, whatsoever state

I am in, therewith to be content. I know both how to be abased, and I know how to abound: Everywhere and in all things, I am instructed both to be full and to be hungry, both to abound and to suffer need. I can do all things through Christ (imagination) who strengthens me" (Phil. 4:11-13).

Paul is the complete embodiment of the state of contentment, and when we embody the state of Paul, we are at home in our reality. Look how Paul starts this passage of scripture, *"Not that I speak in respect of want."* We could also substitute the word "want" with "lack." He knows and believes that he is "one who has" as we spoke of earlier. Being God and knowing he is God, what more could he want? He is not speaking of "wanting" material things.

Paul is speaking with respect to not lacking in the knowledge that he is God. He is in touch with his divine nature. He knows that he is God in human form. The world is his, reality is the clay, and he is the potter. This is the primary issue that haunts people throughout their life — the search for knowing and understanding who they are. Who am I? What is my purpose? What is the meaning of life?

Plainly speaking, constantly trying to find out who we are reveals the state of discontentment in which most of the human race suffers. We are not content because we don't know who we truly are. In this state, we perceive reality as happening to us rather than through us. This is why it is written, *"My people are destroyed for lack of knowledge"* (Hosea 4:6). This is a lack of not knowing who we are that can destroy our creative abilities.

Paul continues and says, "...for I have learned, whatsoever state I am in, therewith to be content." He "learned" to be content and that it is, in fact, a learning process. Some of us pass through various states and never learn, so the same old mental song and dance repeats itself over and over. It can get to the point when someone asks you a simple question like "Hey, how ya doing?" and we respond with something like, "Oh, ya know, same old garbage, different day."

I knew a guy I used to work with several years ago, and when someone would ask him how he was doing, he would respond with, "It's just another turd sandwich on the buffet of life." We've all heard, "Life's a bitch, and then you die." Good grief, is this really all life is to us as God in the flesh?!

All that to say, we need to learn to be content no matter what state we are in. So, what does that really mean? The dictionary definition of "content" is: "A state of peaceful happiness." The Apostle Paul is saying that no matter what physical state he is in (his circumstances), he is grounded in peaceful happiness, and this state of peaceful happiness is our natural, human state of being. The problem is that we have totally forgotten this, and so it must be learned, or perhaps it would be better to say relearned.

Paul, at this point in his life, has been through a lot and so he has learned. We, however, would prefer not to have to go through this learning process, but this is how it tends to work. The furnaces of life are our teachers and their greatest reward is contentment.

You may look back at your life and say something like, "I've been through a lot, more than most people." We always tend to think that we have been through more than others, but actually, everyone goes through the fire, albeit the experience is slightly different for everyone. If you are not content, that just means you haven't learned the lesson yet. True contentment in any state requires nonresistance.

When we resist what is, we push contentment away from us, because the ego loves to resist contentment. Nonresistance is like a magnetic force that pulls contentment toward us while resistance pushes it away. Have you ever taken two magnets, and turned them around in the opposite direction toward each other? When you do this there is a resistance, and you can feel them pushing away from one another.

Nonresistance is simply accepting what is in the present moment and not fighting it. You cannot be content and fight against "what is" at the same time; however, when you are honest with yourself and embrace things as they are, you will find that you naturally begin to ease into contentment.

Embrace your life now exactly as it is with loving awareness. Take a deep, slow breath and relax into it fully. Let all your mental resistance go, even if just for a minute, and accept the present moment. You should feel a sense of relief as you let your guard down and stop fighting life.

This is what Jesus was referring to when he says, *"Ye have heard that it hath been said, an eye for an eye, and a tooth for a tooth: But I say unto you, that you resist not evil: but whosoever shall smite thee on thy right cheek, turn to him the other also"* (Matthew 5:38-39). He is not suggesting here that we should walk around acting like a bunch of cowards by letting people walk over us. Jesus most often uses exaggerated stories as examples to get his point across. Turning the other cheek is simply not fighting against what is.

The point of all this is to fully accept what is and joyfully anticipate your desires manifesting. This is the magic reality creation cocktail, and when you drink it, a quiet confidence sets in, and that feeling of contentment lets you know that you've got this! Contentment is confidence that has settled into a peaceful state of happiness.

It always comes back to knowing who you are. No matter what state you are in, you are God in that state, and that "knowing" is the source of contentment. Without knowing and believing that you are God, contentment is impossible because no matter how prosperous you may be in your physical life, you will always have this sense of something missing, a void. The way we humans operate, we will do everything we can to try and fill that void; however, without the "knowing" nothing will be able to effectively fill it.

I have a friend I've known for over 20 years. We both grew up in the Church and were highly dedicated young Christian warriors! It's funny to think about now, but we were in church every Sunday morning, every Wednesday evening, and often on Saturdays. He ended up going to a large Bible college in our city, and I took a job as a full-time associate minister at one of the fastest-growing megachurches in the country at that time.

We knew the Bible inside and out, and we were well-versed in all the Christian lingo. It's all we ever talked about, but despite all that, something was missing. It always felt that this part of my life was some sort of facade. (And if you also feel that way, trust me; you're not alone.) I loved giving people scripture after scripture to help them with their problems, but I always wondered if it ever did them any good. I had no proof that it actually worked. It never worked all that well for me. No matter how many verses I had memorized, the results were always slim to none.

That's the thing about religions and most churches; they are like riding a bus. Let's say you were going on vacation to the beach, and you decided that you would travel by bus. It will be a long route because you live nowhere near the beach. So, you carefully pack all the things that you're going to need, and then you secure your ticket. The next day, you get on the bus and the journey begins. The bus is crowded with lots of other people who are also going to the beach, and because it's a long ride, you have plenty of time to get to know the other passengers, which you do, and end up becoming friends with many of them.

After a full day of driving, you finally arrive at the beach! It's gorgeous. There is clear blue water, soft white sand, and everyone looks like they're having a wonderful time. Once the bus stops, it's time to get off. But wait, no one is moving. You and everyone else have decided that you're going to stay on the bus. You look out the window and see how beautiful it is. You've arrived at the beach you've traveled so far to get to. Why are you staying on the bus? This doesn't make any sense at all, but for some reason you and everyone else are scared to get off the bus. It's an unreasonable fear—and you know it—but you just can't bring yourself to leave your seat.

Many religions and churches operate just like this. They can take you to a certain point, but when you arrive at your wonderful destination, for God's sake, get off the bus! You are absolutely free to get up, get out, and enjoy the place you've traveled so far to get to.

Here's what happens. When the bus finally arrives at the destination, the exit doors are sticky and hard to open. Then the driver speaks over the microphone, telling everyone that they should probably stay on the bus. It's just too scary out there. Anyway, all your friends are on the bus, and if you just stay in your seat and follow the rules, you'll be safe and sound. The driver then starts asking everyone for money. Gas is expensive after all, and keeping everyone on the bus is a difficult job, so he needs volunteers to help maintain this bus life.

You keep looking out the window and seeing everyone having a wonderful time on the beach—picnicking, flying kites, surfing, and making castles in the sand. They look fearless and look free. Deep inside, you know you're missing out, but you justify never getting off the bus because the driver promises you that it is the best and safest way to live.

If this is you, kick those sticky doors wide open and jump off the bus!

Come on in. The water's fine!

Needless to say, the friend I was talking about has never gotten off the bus. Still, to this day, he mentions that he just doesn't feel as close to God as he should. No matter what he does, no matter how much he goes to church, no matter how much money he puts in the offering plate, he just can't find the inner peace his soul is craving.

I have casually mentioned to him on a few occasions that the gap he feels between himself and God is merely in his mind, and it's only there because he's trying to see God as someone outside of himself. However, he just won't have it, so I don't press the issue. Everyone will eventually wake up and realize their own divinity, and I look forward to the day when my friend makes this discovery.

Paul mentions that he knows "both how to be abased and how to abound." Paul is saying that he knows how to deal with hardships and unwanted circumstances, and he also knows how to be on top of the world, having it all. It's all the same to him because it never changes who he is. In other words, our circumstances don't change who we are. On the contrary, who we are changes our circumstances. We are content when we know who we are since no matter what situation we find ourselves in, we can find God in that situation.

When you know how to do something, then you have confidence and have no fear or anxiety. I'm sure you can think of something that used to make you nervous, but once you experienced doing it, it no longer concerned you.

I remember when I was in my early twenties, I got a job working at a local coffee shop. This place had a $15,000 espresso machine and I was so nervous about using it. After a few shifts, I had it down pat and was making lattes regularly. I even learned how to do latte art, and before long, customers requested that I make their drinks for them. What once scared me became enjoyable, and I learned a new skill along the way!

Once you've been through something, it doesn't scare you anymore—and this is Paul's whole message. Unwanted circumstances don't knock you down because you know in your heart that *"all things are working together for good"* (Romans 8:28, paraphrased).

This truth will anchor you in contentment if you'll let it. Make this the screensaver for your mind. Always remember that ALL things are working together for your good, even if it doesn't look like it. For example, if you get a flat tire on your way to work, your ego will be tempted to ask, "Why did this happen to me? Did I create this reality? Maybe I'm just no good at this. Maybe this reality creation stuff just doesn't work for me." Stop that line of thinking in its tracks! Arrest those thoughts, or simply observe them as they pass through your mind. Realize that everything, including the flat tire, is working together for good. Things like flat tires will happen in life, but what if it kept you from getting in a car wreck later down the road? Who knows? Learn to look at everything as working together for your ultimate good.

When you know that you know that all things are working together for good, then you are in a state of contentment by default. When you are content, you are like Paul who says that whether he is in an undesirable state or a desired state, it doesn't really matter since it doesn't really change anything. These are all just states, and contentment means it's all good, and it's all God, and it's all you. Don't resist yourself. Just be. Know that this too shall pass, as you pass through one state to the next.

Contentment is the fertile soil of reality creation. *"Godliness with content-*

ment is great gain" (1 Timothy 6:6). "Godliness" simply means knowing who you are, God, and when you are content with this "knowing," it produces great gain, and gain means increase. This is the bottom line of negotiating reality. Until we learn to be content with the "here and now," we can't expect the "then and there" to be any different.

When we are content, this causes an increase in consciousness of our divine nature, which will organically bring increase into our experience of reality. Contentment is the cause. Gain is the effect.

The state of contentment is the state of reality creation. It does not mean that we restrain our desires because we are simply happy with what we have. We can be happy and at peace regardless of what we have or don't have because we know we are God, and God is always expanding and creating. So, let's be content creators!

CONTENTMENT EXERCISE: MANTRA ROLLING

A mantra is a word, statement, or phrase repeated over and over, which aids in focusing the mind. A mantra is a wonderful way to embed your subconscious mind with a new thought or idea and when practiced regularly it will begin to project into your reality.

Mantra rolling is allowing the mantra to roll on an endless loop in your mind. You can do this at any time throughout the day—at work, mowing the yard, cleaning the house or even as you're drifting off to sleep. You can do this whenever and wherever you desire. It's simple, fun, and effective.

The mantra for this exercise is: "All things are working together for good."

Say the mantra out loud several times where you can hear yourself. Now, say it a few times quietly to yourself and then switch to silently saying it in your mind. This gets the mantra rolling. Hear it playing over and over in your mind for as long as you like. After a while, it will become a default program that runs in your subconscious. As you are out and about, and something either good, bad, or indifferent happens, your natural response to the situation will be "all things are working together for good." You will feel content in knowing this and will be able to continue creating without interference from unexpected circumstances.

"Great things are done when men and mountains meet."

\- William Blake

CHAPTER 9
THE TONGUE

Words are a type of portable magic since they allow us a glimpse behind the invisible veil into the reality of one's heart and mind, the source of all creation. It's a difficult task, if not impossible, to express the sheer power of words by using words. It is sufficient to say that words are the lifeblood of reality creation.

The Bible is often referred to as the "Word of God," which, on one level, it is. In reality, all words are the word of God, not just the ones bound between two pieces of leather. You are God, I am God, we are God, and every time we speak, it is the word of God. We are either giving life or taking it away.

"Death and life are in the power of the tongue" (Proverbs 18:21). We have all of God's power at our disposal; what we do with it is entirely up to us. Kind of spooky, isn't it? If you understand that every time you speak, it is God speaking, then for God's sake, be mindful about what you say about yourself and others. It's God speaking about God. The fabric of

your reality is sewn together by your words, and you need to be aware that it can also be ripped apart at the seams by them as well.

With this in mind, we need to be observant of the inner dialogue we have going on within ourselves. We all engage in an ongoing conversation between our higher (spirit) and lower (ego) selves. Older vintage cartoons used to portray this with characters like Bugs Bunny, Porky Pig, Yosemite Sam, and so forth. They would have a haloed angel on one shoulder and a little pitchfork-wielding devil on the other.

Whenever one of these characters faced a difficult decision, usually a moral one, the angel and the devil would appear. The devil would always say something like, "Go ahead, Porky, take that fresh apple pie off grandma's windowsill. You know you want to." Then the angel would appear and say something like, "Now, Porky, you don't really want to take that pie from that sweet old lady, do you?" The conversation would go back and forth with this dialogue until, finally, a decision was made, and the angel always seemed to win out.

I'm not saying that your lower self is a devil and your higher self is an angel, but you get the point. We all have a similar dialogue going on inside us. It's a type of inner talking, and we all do it. Sometimes this inner talking is even spoken out loud and usually happens when we're alone. Do you ever notice yourself talking to yourself when no one is around? Do you ever notice how sometimes this talking is negative and pessimistic?

The more self-aware we become, the more we are able to observe this dialogue from the perspective of a witness instead of a participant. It's a wonderful idea to excuse yourself from the drama of life every now and then, step off the stage and take a seat in the audience, and just observe this play of life. Observe how you think and speak about yourself. What you discover may surprise you. Death and life are in the power of the tongue.

Are your words giving you life or are they taking it away?

There has been much research and scientific experimentation that shows how powerful our words are. One such experiment was performed by Masaru Emoto, a Japanese pseudoscientist whose findings show that our words can have a dramatic effect on the molecular structure of water. The experiment was a simple one: He took two containers of water and, over the course of several days, he spoke positive words to one and negative words to the other. After several days past, he took both containers and placed them in a freezer. Once both containers were frozen solid, he removed them from the freezer and simply observed them, the results were staggering! The water in both containers had frozen into ice. However, the one that had positive words spoken to it had frozen into beautiful geometric, artistic-looking patterns and shapes, while the other one that had negative words spoken to it turned into ugly, misshapen patterns and designs. There was such an obvious difference between the two.

You can test the power of your words by conducting your own experiments from home. If you have a couple of houseplants, you can place an index card with positive words on one plant and another card with negative words on the other plant. After several weeks, you should notice a difference between the two. One will look healthy and vibrant, while the other will look wilted. You can do the same thing with two glasses of water. Speak positive words to one and speak negative words to the other. One will taste clean and refreshing, while the other one won't taste nearly as good.

Now, here's the interesting thing: According to the latest research, our human bodies are at least 60% water. That's more than half. We are literally a "body of water." This is precisely why we don't feel very good when around a bunch of negativity. The negative words deform the molecular structure of the water inside our bodies. This is especially true when it comes to negative self-talk. We need to become aware of this and change the dialogue to a positive one so that we're speaking life to ourselves and not draining it away. We shouldn't let others belittle us with their words, either. If we find ourselves in such a situation, we can be nonresistant and politely excuse ourselves from the conversation.

There is a very powerful technique known as "pre-paving" that can help us avoid being caught in a potentially negative situation. Pre-paving is especially useful when it comes to "routine" negativity, like being around negative family members, friends, or coworkers.

Pre-paving involves using your imagination ahead of an event and laying the foundation before a negative situation occurs. Essentially, this allows you to stay one step ahead. For instance, maybe you have dinner once a week at your mother's house, and she is a "negative Nancy." The conversation may start out fine, but it's inevitable that it will take a turn toward the negative. And once she gets riled up, all hell can break loose...literally! *"And the tongue is a fire, a world of iniquity: so is the tongue among our members, that it defileth the whole body, and setteth on fire the course of nature; and it is set on fire of hell"* (James 3:6).

As we discussed earlier in the book, there is no actual hell, this passage is referring to how our words can create a "hell on earth" type of situation. So, here's what you can do *before* you go to dinner. The day before, pause and use your imagination to see the evening with Mom going as you would like it to go. See everything as you desire it to be: a lovely meal and a lovely conversation. Try to bring in all the tones of reality. What does the food smell like? How does your mom greet you at the door? Where is everyone sitting at the table? What dishes is she serving the food on? What do you talk about? What do you not talk about? How do you say goodbye after dinner? See yourself driving back home with a smile because it was such a lovely evening! Feel that feeling! Stay in this moment in your imagination until it feels right to let it go.

The next day, as you prepare to go to dinner, have absolute confidence in your reality negotiating skills. Fully expect the evening to go exactly as you saw it in your mind's eye. You have laid the foundation ahead of time, and if you remain loyal to your imaginal act, it will project into your reality. Because all of eternity is contained in the present moment, it can be as if the years of negative get-togethers with your mom never actually happened! No one will know what has transpired except for you. A mountain was cast into the sea. You did this in the secret place of your imagination, and you have been rewarded openly. Good on you!

The beautiful thing about using your creative imagination to pre-pave a future event, especially one that has a high likelihood of involving negative talk like the above scenario, is that you are laying the foundation ahead of time for everyone involved to use their words wisely and in a compassionate and loving manner, which in turn will have a positive effect on everyone's state of mind. In essence, we are assuming the mind of Christ for ourselves and others, and by doing so, we are creating an environment where life-giving words are both spoken and heard.

Scripture tells us in the book of Hebrews 4:12, *"The word of God is quick, and powerful, and sharper than any two-edged sword, piercing even to the dividing asunder of soul and spirit, and of the joints and marrow, and is a discerner of the thoughts and intents of the heart."*

This is powerful stuff, and this is who you are! Your words are all those things described in the above verse. You can bring out the best in people with your words, but you can also bring out the worst in them. You can wound, and you can heal. You can kill, and you can make alive. With your words, you can pull a person out of a particular negative state and place them in a positive one. I am sure you have noticed how certain words make you feel.

The Bible says, *"A soft answer turneth away wrath: but grievous words stir up anger"* (Proverbs 15:1). We can test the truth of this verse every day by responding to those around us with soft answers. When someone around you is in a state of anger, try softly responding to the anger and see what happens. The odds are that you will witness them change states.

Your ego will perceive your softness as weakness, but it is not weakness; it is meekness, and there is a world of difference between the two. Weakness is power(less), meekness is power(full). Meekness simply means "power under control," and this power is the power of God, which is under the control of your words. *"Blessed are the meek, for they shall inherit the earth"* (Matthew 5:5).

The entire earth and everything in it belongs to you, and you inherit it by using your words. Every day, we have countless opportunities to negotiate our reality by intentionally using our words. Each one of us lives in our unique world, no two being exactly alike. If someone around us is sad or depressed, we can speak life-giving words of encouragement to them and in so doing, help to pull them out of the state they have fallen into. Don't be timid or afraid to do this. Remind yourself of how powerful your words are. Keep Hebrews 4:12 in your back pocket at all times.

Your words are powerful, so if you feel like you have a message in your heart for someone, by all means, deliver that message. Perhaps it's just a simple "I love you" or "I've been thinking about you," or maybe it's something deeper than that, something you've been meaning to tell someone for a long time, like how much they mean to you, or that you're grateful that they're in your life. It could be a phone call you've been meaning to make or maybe an apology you've been hanging on to for far too long. Your words can be life-changing, and this is one of the ways that life happens through you.

Why not resurrect the ancient art of letter writing? No emails or texts allowed. Actually write a letter to someone, put a stamp on it, walk to the mailbox and mail it. Your words in handwritten form are like pure magic. Free from the constraints of time, they are eternal—something that was once in the invisible realm of your human heart is now drawn out and put onto paper in this physical reality...magic! You never really know the impact you can make on those people who are in your life through the power of words.

"In the beginning was the word, and the word was with God, and the word was God" (John 4:11), *"And God said, let there be light, and there was light"* (Genesis 1:3). This is how God (you) created reality, and this is how God (you) continues to create reality, by speaking words of life and letting them be. Let there be...

Speak like the God you are, so place intention behind your words: "Let there be love in my life, let there be peace in my life, let there be good health in my life, let there be joy and happiness in my life, let there be contentment in my life, let there be mystical experiences in my life, let there be prosperity in my life, let there be passionate sex in my life, let there be____________" and you name it. Speak whatever you desire to be manifested in your reality.

Speak it, feel it, be it.

Start by speaking what's in your heart because your mind needs to hear what's in there, and the only way it can do that is if it comes out of your mouth. This is crucial for your mind to get on board because your mind cannot truly believe in something unless you speak it out of your mouth. This is the power of words.

"With the heart man believeth unto righteousness; and with the mouth confession is made unto salvation" (Romans 10:10). In this instance, we can also say, "confession is made unto manifestation."

It's a simple three-step process that will change your life forever. Heart-Mouth-Mind. That's it, and precisely in that order. It will not work any other way. This is how you follow your heart and create the reality you desire. If you try to mix up the steps, you will fail. When you're not following your heart, you often end up following someone else's plan for your life. Whether or not it is the "right thing," it will never feel right to you because it came from someone other than yourself.

Heart-Mouth-Mind. A belief or desire in the human heart has to come out of the mouth before it can enter the mind, where reality is created. This is crucial because living from your heart is the only way to find true satisfaction.

When the mind latches onto something in the heart, heart-mind coherence is established, and our inner desires begin to manifest in our reality. It's a funny thing, but you literally need to hear yourself speak what's in your heart. Let's look at that scripture one more time and notice how it reveals this ancient three-step process. *"With the heart, man believeth unto righteousness [you believe in your heart, which causes right thinking] and with the mouth, confession is made unto salvation"* (Romans 10:10). "Salvation" simply means the answer, the solution, the manifestation. So, when you confess with your mouth what is in your heart, when you hear yourself say it, then it creates the solution, the answer, salvation.

For instance, perhaps you've been going back and forth in your mind about your current relationship. Part of you thinks that you should try to be happy. The person you are with has many good qualities, and they may even be a great person. However, something in your heart just doesn't feel right. This starts to eat you up, and you continue going back and forth in your mind. Should you stay together or should you break up? This state of indecision starts to make you feel sick. The mental anguish is now causing physical side effects. You just don't know what to do.

Here's the solution: Simply speak out loud whatever the dominant feeling in your heart is. You know what it is—yes, you do. You know what it is. You're just scared to hear yourself say it. But if you want peace in your life, you have to say it. So say it. Scream it if you need to. Cry it if you need to. It is difficult to admit what's in your heart, and the reason why it is difficult is because it's the truth. The truth is in your heart. Sometimes we think we can't handle the truth, but that's just the ego talking. If we're going to live authentic lives and follow our hearts, we have to be honest with ourselves about what our hearts are telling us. It may be scary to hear yourself say it, but once you do, you will be liberated! So say it! Speak the dominant feeling in your heart, even if it's 49%—51%, you know which feeling has the edge. Say it.

Tears will often stream down your face as a deep sense of relief floods every cell of your body. All is well because now, for perhaps the first time, you are following your heart. How is this possible? It's possible because you heard yourself say it. You brought the invisible truth from inside your heart and gave it life in your reality by speaking it out of your mouth. Once you hear it, it enters your mind and creates right thinking, and with this, you have begun to follow your heart.

Heart-Mouth-Mind. It has to come from you, because no one else in the world can say what's in your heart. Even if they could, your mind wouldn't register it as the truth because it didn't come from you.

Whatever you do, don't skip a step or take them out of order. If you know something is in your heart and you try to direct it straight to your mind without allowing it to come out of your mouth, you will enter a state of indecision, and this can be hard to escape. Unfortunately, people do this all the time. Instead of following their hearts and being honest with themselves, they try to follow their minds. Because they are in a state of indecision, they become increasingly confused.

The moment the truth of the heart is confessed with the mouth, salvation appears. Right thinking establishes itself in your mind, and you start following your heart, creating your desires, and negotiating reality.

Heart-Mouth-Mind is the mystical three-step process that can change your world forever. So simple, so powerful, so healing, and yet often ignored; but not by you, not anymore! The magic elevator that creates reality has three floors at which it stops:

1st floor - Heart
2nd floor - Mouth
3rd floor - Mind

Make sure to always stop at these three sequential floors, and you will always be following your heart, which will always bring you the best life.

"This is the covenant that I will make with them after those days, saith the Lord, I will put my laws into their hearts, and in their minds will I write them" (Hebrews 10:16). The covenant is "imagination creates reality," and

we see the heart and mind principle at work here. The covenant is in our heart, it comes out of the mouth of God (our mouth), and then it gets written in our mind.

From this point, we can begin to speak words of affirmation. Affirmations are very popular these days, and for good reason. They produce results—however, to get these results, affirmations must be spoken from within the completed imaginative act. In other words, you create the reality you desire in your mind. Create it all the way through to the end, and from this place, begin speaking affirmations confirming the fact that it's a done deal. If done properly, you should be able to feel the very real feeling of accomplishment and completion. As these affirming words of truth roll off your tongue, they are literally dripping with creative energy.

Affirmations are simply affirming what has already been created, and they are a great ally in helping you "keep the faith" during the waiting period of your manifestation. It is: *"Calling those things which be not as though they were"* (Romans 4:17). We could also say it is: "Speaking like we can see the things we cannot see." Remember the words of William Blake, "Everything that is seen was once only imagined."

For example, let's say you have a desire to move to a new home. You can see it vividly in your imagination. You know the location. You can see the floor plan, you can feel the wood floors under your feet, you can see the view from the kitchen window, you can smell your favorite candle burning in the living room, and life is good in this home. From this point of completion, you would begin to speak your affirmations, such as: "It feels great to be a homeowner," "I just love my new home," "I'm so happy here in our new town," "My family loves being here in our new house."

Your affirmations should come naturally to you. They should be organic, not manufactured. Don't try to force any affirmation that doesn't feel natural to you, because feeling is the secret. You can even fall asleep at night saying these affirmations in your head; this is a wonderful practice, and from time to time you will be rewarded with dreams of being in your new home, which will serve to bolster your faith in your reality negotiating skills. Also, don't forget that this is supposed to be fun—you can even make your affirmations rhyme from time to time.

You are speaking from the point of "one who has" and so to you "more will be given." You are God speaking, and when God speaks, their words carry a lot of weight, all the weight of the universe, so much so that we read, *"So shall my word be that goeth forth out of my mouth: it shall not return unto me void, but it shall accomplish that which I please, and it shall prosper in the thing whereto I sent it"* (Isaiah 55:11). Let this truth sink in for a minute. Your words are extremely powerful! When you speak, it is the word of God, and your words will not return to you void, but they will accomplish what you sent them to do.

"Let the weak say, I am strong" (Joel 3:10). These words cannot return void. When you say "I AM" this is the name of God, and whatever you say after that will come to pass. You are speaking from the point of completion, from the end. Even though you can't see it yet, you know that you already have what you're affirming. *"We walk by faith and not by sight"* (2 Cor. 5:7). It's easy to believe things we can see, but it takes faith to believe we have what we cannot see. *"Blessed are they that have not seen and yet have believed"* (John 20:29). Blessed with what? Blessed with what you believe you have. Believe it before you see it, and then you'll see it. Affirmations help you maintain the proper mental state during the obligatory gestation period of your manifestation.

"For the vision is yet for an appointed time, but at the end it shall speak, and

not lie: though it tarry, wait for it; because it will surely come..." (Habakkuk 2:3). Isn't it interesting how this is worded? *"At the end it shall speak."* When we use affirmations, we are speaking from the end. I cannot stress this enough: we must live and affirm from the end of our creative act. If you created a new home in your imagination and you are still sleeping in your current home in your physical reality, sleep as though you were in your new home. As your head hits the pillow every night, feel it as though it is your new pillow, on your new bed, in your new home. Fall asleep night after night in the mental reality of your new home, and one day, before too long, you will be waking up in your new home. That's living from the end. *"Wait for it, because it will surely come."*

William Blake said, "Great things happen when men and mountains meet," and Jesus said, *"Say unto this mountain, be thou removed and be thou cast into the sea"* (Mark 11:23). Are there things that seem to be standing in the way of your desired reality? Remove these mountains in your imagination and speak to them in your physical reality as if they are already moving, and they will have no choice but to move out of your way. You can move mountains for yourself and others because your words are law. Always remember that the universe has your back!

AFFIRMATION EXERCISE

Create a scene in your mind that represents your desire fully realized. This can be absolutely anything, and it can be for yourself or someone else. As an example, let's say that you desire a promotion at work. What would the end of that look like? It would probably involve your fellow co-workers shaking your hand and congratulating you on a job well done. Put yourself in the scene from a first-person perspective. You are not merely seeing yourself receiving a handshake, rather, you are actually shaking hands with them—feel your hand in theirs and hear them congratulating you. This is just an example. The idea is to create a scene that feels natural and organic for your particular situation.

Now, create an affirmation that speaks from the end. Again, something that feels natural, something you would actually say if your desire was realized. It needs to "click." For example, something like, "Damn, it feels so good to get that promotion. I worked hard and it finally paid off!"

You can repeat this affirmation as many times as you like throughout the day. Many people get wonderful results from repeating it in their mind as they drift off to sleep. This helps to make an impression on your subconscious, which will eventually project outward in your reality.

"The imagination is not a state,
it is the human experience itself."

- William Blake

CHAPTER 10

FIRST FRUITS

"Again, the kingdom of heaven is like unto a treasure hidden in a field: the which when a man hath found, he hideth, and for joy thereof goeth and selleth all that he hath, and buyeth that field" (Matthew 13:44).

This is perhaps the most beautiful passage in all of scripture. The kingdom of heaven is like a treasure hidden in a field. Now, we know the kingdom of heaven is within us. It's not a separate place somewhere beyond the clouds that we get to go to someday if we make the grade. It is within us, and it is your wonderful human imagination.

It's remarkable how grossly misunderstood the Bible is, and to make matters worse, these misunderstandings are shared with masses of people every Sunday morning around the world. I used to be right there with them, and I've preached the same contradicting messages from my own mouth. I did it for years! I used to get angry about this, but as my awareness of God expanded, I learned to have compassion for everyone, knowing that in their own perfect time, they, too, will come into the knowledge of the truth.

At some point, everyone on the planet will see clearly, and in the meantime, we simply must love, serve, and remember that we were once wrestling with the truth ourselves just as they are wrestling with it now. We are all one, and to extend love and understanding toward another human being is to extend it to yourself.

"Tat Tvam Asi." This is a Hindu saying that means, "I am that too." The great spiritual teacher Ram Dass spoke about this nearly every day of his life, and he did more than talk about it—he practiced it. He had learned to see everyone as part of himself, so his life became the embodiment of pure, holy love. This coincides with Neville Goddard's idea that the entire universe is only yourself pushed out.

"I am that too" helps to keep things in perspective, especially when dealing with unpleasant people. They are simply in a temporary state, and we have been there too. Jesus said that the entire Bible could be summed up in one sentence, *"For the entire law is fulfilled in one word, even in this; Thou shalt love thy neighbor as thyself"* (Galatians 5:14). The word "neighbor" here simply refers to your fellow human beings since we are all neighbors in this shared human experience. The only way we can truly love our neighbors is if we can see our neighbors as ourselves.

The kingdom of heaven is within us, and it's like a treasure hidden in a field. Remarkably, Jesus uses these particular words to describe the kingdom. Science has now proven the existence of the quantum field, where all potentials and variables exist. The kingdom of heaven, where all things are possible, is the quantum field. We access it in the present moment, the now, where everything and nothing exists simultaneously. This "field" is where the treasure of your imagination is hidden. No wonder we're instructed to *"Seek ye first the kingdom of God and his righteousness, and all these things shall be added unto you"* (Matthew 6:33). If we have access to a place where everything is possible, wouldn't it make sense to go there first?

Ephesians 3:20-21says, *"Now unto him that is able to do exceedingly abundantly above all that we ask or think, according to the power that worketh in us."* This is you. Your higher Self (God) is able to do exceedingly above anything your normal or lower self could possibly ask or think. Because Jesus Christ (your imagination) is in the quantum field where all possibilities exist, nothing is impossible for you!

The idea of *seeking the kingdom of God first* is a common theme that runs throughout scripture, and it makes perfect sense if you understand why. But even this idea has been misunderstood so that we're left with the impression that "God" is some sort of attention seeker that gets Its feelings hurt and may even turn Its back on us if we don't give It the attention It deserves. Sadly, this is the impression so many people have because that's what has been preached over the years.

So, how exactly do we seek the kingdom first? Well, on the base level, we become present. Most people are not fully present in today's world. We are too distracted by life, and it's really difficult to be present when we're all constantly on our phones. There are, of course, exceptions to this, like when we're on FaceTime with a friend or family member or being present in a current conversation. I'm not saying cellphones are bad or good. They just are. The more you expand your consciousness, the more the knowledge of good and evil dissipates, and you begin to see things as they really are: just things being things.

However, this does not change the fact that our lives are filled with dis tractions, full of things that extract our attention from the now. Many of us have our attention on hypothetical situations, things that may or may not ever happen. Some of us have our attention on the past, things that happened a very long time ago, and they're still distracting us to this day. Many of us have our attention on social media because we simply cannot live without knowing what our friends and total strangers are up to today. We must know!

Where our attention goes, our energy flows. Negotiating reality requires energy and presence, and when we are focused on everything besides the here and now, there is no energy to create in the moment. So, our lives run the same old program day in and day out—the same old stuff, different day.

You've probably heard the famous Albert Einstein quote, "The definition of insanity is doing the same thing over and over but expecting different results," and by this definition, over half the world must be insane! Have you ever wondered why we use the phrase *paying attention*? We say these words because we inherently know that it's costing us something, and what it's costing us is our creative energy. When we are focused on anything outside the present moment, the price is our creative energy.

The kingdom of God (your creative imagination) is the source of your reality, and the Bible says that if we seek this first, "all these things will be added unto us." What are "all these things?" Well, that's up to you. It can quite literally be anything you could ask or think. If we don't enter our imagination first when attempting to negotiate reality, we are bound to be tossed around by life, and that's not a very fulfilling way to live.

Can you imagine taking a road trip without knowing what direction you should go? Just driving around willy-nilly day after day, week after week, you'd never make it to your destination and may even end up in some places you had no business going. This would be very frustrating. It's like that scene in the movie *Dumb and Dumber*, where Harry and Lloyd are supposed to be driving to Aspen, Colorado, but instead, they drive hundreds of miles in the wrong direction. Harry wakes up and looks out the window and says, "Huh, I thought the Rocky Mountains would be a little rockier than this. That John Denver is full of shit, man!" That scene cracks me up! But, as funny as it is, we don't want to go through life with zero direction. It's like the old saying by Zig Ziglar, "If you aim at nothing, you'll hit it every time."

One of the benefits of seeking the kingdom first is a sense of direction. Seeking the kingdom first leads to righteousness (right thinking), and if we're thinking right, then we're not fumbling through life like *Dumb and Dumber*. There have certainly been times when I was not seeking the kingdom first, had no direction, and my wife and I were like Harry and Lloyd, manifesting one dumb thing after another. We've all been there, smack dab in the middle of the law of opposites, which goes like this: "Do not seek the kingdom of God first, and nothing you desire will be added unto you." That's not a fun place to be.

"In all thy ways acknowledge him and he shall direct thy path" (Proverbs 3:6). The "him" in this verse is Jesus Christ (your imagination). Before we do anything, make any decision, start something new, or even wake up on a new day, we should acknowledge him by going into our imagination, for it is here that we will receive direction for our path.

You are the author and the finisher of your life story. Use your imagination and lay out your path before you. See in your mind's eye where you want to go, and the quantum field will produce the steps that appear along your path. Trust your imagination and stay loyal to it.

The things you create with your imagination are real before they appear in your physical reality. If you have an important decision to make, such as moving, a new career path, or a new relationship, go into your imagination and see all the possible scenarios and how each one could play out. This is the quantum field, and you arrange and rearrange the subatomic particles of every possible outcome. When you see the desired outcome in your mind, select that potential, and it becomes your way. This is the direction that you receive from acknowledging "him." The particles become waves, and you surf that wave into your desired reality. With God, all things are possible.

Direction is not the only thing we receive when we seek the kingdom first. We see in Malachi 3:10: *"Bring ye all the tithes into the storehouse, that there may be meat in mine house, and prove me now herewith, saith the Lord of hosts, if I will not open you the windows of heaven, and pour you out a blessing, that there shall not be room enough to receive it."*

Boy, oh boy, this is one scripture that the Church has definitely hijacked. Many Churches have literally taken this so far out of context that you can't even recognize it anymore. They have built tax-free empires and have controlled masses of people, herding them like cattle, or "sheep," as they like to refer to them, through their misinterpretation—which, in turn, morphs into financial brainwashing on a global scale.

This scripture has not a thing in the world to do with giving the church 10% of your hard-earned income. The "tithe" is the "first fruits," or we could say "first thoughts." Tithing is seeking the kingdom of God first by bringing your first thoughts about anything you want to accomplish into your imagination instead of just immediately running out and trying to make things happen with human effort. We need to seek the kingdom first, then create what we desire with the power and wisdom of God rather than just letting the chips fall where they may.

The "storehouse" and the "house" referred to in this passage of scripture is your imagination. The Church hijacked these words and made them their own by falsely claiming that the Church itself is the house of God, but nothing could be further from the truth. *"God that made the world and all things therein, seeing that he is Lord of heaven and earth, dwelleth not in temples made with hands"* (Acts 17:24). And again, *"What? Know ye not that your body is the temple of the holy ghost..."* (1 Cor. 6:19). So hopefully that clears things up. You are the house of God, not the organized Church! The tithe is your first thoughts. The storehouse is your imagination. So bring your first thoughts into your imagination so that there will be food in there. Brain food. Food for thought, something to work with.

Now, this is where it gets interesting. God says to test him in this. If we are told to test something, then we are asked to find out if it is a surety, a law. The first fruits principle will never fail for it opens the windows of heaven over you. In other words, following this universal law causes your desires to manifest from within the quantum field. Your first thoughts organize themselves in such a way that it causes them to materialize as physical things in your reality.

This process allows reality to be negotiable from your point of view. We all have individualized viewpoints of God, but if we don't abide by the first thoughts principle and go about trying to change things from matter to matter, it becomes very difficult and unnecessarily challenging to live an abundant life. It can be done, but the effort involved and the amount of time it takes cause most people to give up along the way, which results in a life of struggle and "just barely getting by."

Abundant life is described in this verse, blessings pouring out on you, so much so that you won't even be able to receive them all. *"I am come that they may have life, and that they might have it more abundantly"* (John 10:10). The sole purpose of Jesus Christ (your imagination) is to give you abundant life. If you're unsure about this, just test it, like the verse says. What have you got to lose? We all have goals in life, and it doesn't matter what they are, big or small, strange or bizarre. *"...God is no respecter of persons"* (Acts 10:34). Enter your imagination first before you do anything else, first thoughts in hand, and create the reality you desire. When you do, you will accomplish things beyond your wildest dreams, beyond more than you ever thought you could. After all, as Einstein said, "Imagination is more important than knowledge." Test this law. If you don't get the results you desire, you can always go back to doing whatever it was you were doing before. But first, test it.

"A man's heart deviseth his way: but the Lord directeth his steps" (Proverbs 16:9). This verse speaks of taking the desires of our heart to the Lord (imagination), and then, in a way we know not of, the steps to its manifestation unfold before us. Make this your method of operation for everything you do, big or small, and you will naturally be directed to its realization. In other words, you will walk right into your manifested desires.

For many years, before I understood this principle, I would make plans and get all excited about them, only to be discouraged when they didn't work out. I would come up with fantastic ideas that I thought could never fail. Yet, more often than not, they did fail. Success rarely came, but I did have a nice collection of halfway manifested desires.

It's simply not enough just to make plans. If you don't create the reality of those plans with Jesus Christ (imagination) then they're just plans, and they will remain plans until somebody does something about them. There's nothing more disheartening than someone else taking your plans and having great success with them while you sit on the sidelines and watch. It's devastating, and it leads to an uncreative life of sadness where nothing ever seems to work out.

An unfulfilled life is not what we came here for. We came to have life and live more abundantly, and we can most assuredly do that; however, it does not come from giving 10% of your income to an organization masquerading around as the house of God. Abundant life comes from us taking our first thoughts to the Lord and letting him direct our steps. This is the path. We did not sign up for this human incarnation to wander around this planet aimlessly with no direction. It doesn't matter where you are in life, or whether you are rich or poor, whether you are sick or healthy, young or old, start using the Heart-Mouth-Mind first fruits principle right now, and this very moment, things will start to change from the inside out.

OPEN THE WINDOWS OF HEAVEN MEDITATION

Duration: 20 Minutes

Find a place where you can sit quietly for twenty minutes. Close your eyes. Breathe in deeply and slowly, in through the nose, out through the mouth. Repeat this breath for approximately two minutes. Feel a sense of calm enveloping you.

Settle into this relaxed state and say to yourself, "The windows of heaven are open over me."

Now, allow what's in your heart to slowly rise up to your mouth, something that you've been afraid to admit, but you know it's true. Let it rise, and have the courage to speak it aloud now. You are releasing something that you've been holding in your heart for too long. It's taken a lot of your energy to keep it there all this time. Speak the truth that is in your heart, whatever it may be. If you feel like crying, this is normal. Let it out. Once you have spoken your truth, sit with it quietly for two minutes. Visualize the windows of heaven opening in the space above your head. Feel the unconditional love falling down on you like warm summer rain. God (your higher Self) is raining love down on you because you have taken this time to honor your true divine nature. You are being saturated with unconditional love, inside and out. Soak it in. Feel it. When you are ready, slowly open your eyes.

"Folly is an endless maze; tangled roots perplex her ways."

- William Blake

CHAPTER 11
FOCUS POCUS

As previously mentioned, where our attention goes, our energy flows, so we could say that our focus determines our reality. The word "focus" means the center of our interest or activity. When I look back on my life, the problem was not so much a lack of focus as trying to focus on too many things at one time, and unfortunately, this is what a lot of people do.

Contrary to popular belief, I really don't think we're designed to be multi-tasking all the time, and because of this, I think it's safe to say that many of us are "Jacks of all trades, masters of none." This may be great for becoming part of the system, but it's not ideal for negotiating reality. We came here to be so much more than just a cog in the machine. It's of no real benefit for us to know a little about a lot, but it's extremely beneficial for us to know a lot about one thing in particular.

Whenever you see someone excelling at something in life, it's a direct result of their focused attention. Likewise, when you see someone succumb to something that is undesirable, it's almost always directly related to the person's focus on that issue.

I am speaking from experience here—I'm not just theorizing. My childhood consisted of my father focusing on his art career and my mother focusing on her writing. They both achieved success in their areas of focus; however, my mother eventually stopped focusing on her poetry and started focusing all her attention on her diabetes.

My mother was diagnosed with type one diabetes when she was nine years old, and I was born when she was in her early twenties. She always took really good care of herself when she was younger, and though she had this disease, her focus was always on being creative and writing poetry. She rarely had any health issues and lived a pretty normal life. You wouldn't have ever known that she was diabetic. Sadly, that normalcy began to fade as she started to fully identify with having a terminal disease.

When my mother had completely stopped focusing on her passion for writing, her life became a story of sickness and ever-declining health over a period of several years. You could tell that her focus had shifted because this disease became all she ever talked about. Every day there was some new ailment she focused on, and eventually these ailments intensified to the point of no return. Where your attention goes, your energy flows. She gave so much attention to her disease that it eventually consumed every last drop of her energy. She passed away in her early fifties from diabetes complications.

I loved my mother dearly and still miss her. Though her life story did not have a very happy ending, it taught me a valuable lesson: When you focus on something negative, bad things can happen. Negative attention creates a negative reality.

Have you ever noticed that what you focus on starts to pop up more regularly in your reality? For example, say you've been thinking about buying a car, and you've been watching videos and researching a certain make and model, say a Tesla. The next thing you know, you're seeing Teslas everywhere you go. It's funny how this works. Since you've been focusing your attention on a Tesla for a while, now it seems like everyone and their dog is driving one!

This law of focus applies to absolutely everyone and everything. For example, if we focus on our lack of money, it will be a lack of money that keeps showing up in our reality. You've heard the phrase, "The rich keep getting richer, and the poor keep getting poorer." This is due to the law of focus. Generally, wealthy people are focused on being wealthy, and poor people are generally focused on their lack of wealth, so the same cycle keeps repeating itself, and it will continue until the focus shifts. Now, I'm not trying to make this all about money because that's definitely not what this book is about, but it is one commonality that we all must deal with in life, and as such, it's something that we can all identify with.

I am in no way suggesting that you should ignore what seems to be, but I am suggesting that we shouldn't focus too much on something if it's negative. For instance, you wake up with a crick in your neck, and you notice it; maybe you pop a few ibuprofens and go about your day, and before you know it, the pain is gone. Alternatively, if you keep focusing on the pain and complaining about it all day, it tends to get worse and worse.

When we're not content, we tend to focus on the negative aspects of our reality, which breeds more discontent and unhappiness. It's almost as if, by default, we focus on what we don't have rather than on what we do have. Quite often, a shift in focus is all we need to alter our reality for the better.

Instead of waking up and immediately focusing on how small our house is, what a bummer our job is, or how irritating our ex-wife or ex-husband is, we can shift our focus. This is what we were talking about earlier: When we change the way we look at things, the things we look at change. Try it out! Put this to the test!

Make a deal with yourself. When you wake up tomorrow morning, simply look at the things you have instead of focusing on what you don't have. Love and appreciate everything that you have now, in this present moment. By doing this, you are seeing from the perspective of your higher Self. You are accepting the "now" for what it is, and the "now" is exactly where you're supposed to be. Try to conjure up a little gratitude (even if it's difficult) as you look at what you have. Swap out the automatic complaining with a "Thank you!"

Seeing things from a higher perspective allows you to perceive reality as negotiable. Being grateful for what you already have opens the door for an increase in abundance, almost as if it's making room for it. Expanding your awareness of what you have now, in this moment, automatically expands your capacity to receive more.

If you could see beyond the veil, you'd be amazed at how much space and energy complaining about your present situation occupies. So, for the next day, try to only focus only on the positive aspects of your life. Even if you think these things are small and insignificant, be grateful. When you focus on the positive, no matter how big or small, your energy flows to it, and it intensifies.

Sometimes when we find ourselves in undesirable circumstances, it can be hard to find something positive to focus on, but there's always something... like your dog, for instance. Maybe you have a great relationship with your dog, and they love you unconditionally. They are always happily waiting for you to get home from work. Great! Focus on that. As you do this, your relationship with your dog will expand. You will enjoy each other's company even more, and your normal everyday walk in the park will seem like a whole new experience!

As your relationship and the unconditional love you share with your dog expand, your vibrational frequency increases, which in turn attracts more unconditional love into your field of perception. Now, more good things will be attracted into your reality, all because you shifted your focus. So, will you try it?

When you alter your focus and it produces feelings of gratitude from within, you place yourself in a state of receivership, and situations and events appear in your reality that produce more things to be grateful for. Your reality is like a magnetic mirror that reflects and attracts positively or negatively depending on your focus.

One example of the power of focus is a camera. Focusing causes the image of reality in the lens to become clear, allowing you to look at something far away or up close. It may appear blurry at first, but when you adjust the focus, it becomes sharp and clear. Your attention is like a camera. You can point your attention at anything you wish, and when you focus that attention, its reality becomes clear.

The problem arises when we try to focus on too many things at once, which causes everything to remain blurry. We simply aren't designed to focus hard on numerous things at one time. We can, however, keep multiple things in our field of perception using a technique known as "soft focusing."

Have you ever seen one of those Magic Eye books from the late 1980s? There was a hidden image in the middle of the pages, but you couldn't see it by simply looking at it. Instead, you had to blur the page with soft focus, and then the main image would pop out right in front of you. Your imagination is like a Magic Eye, but what you see is totally up to you.

Soft focusing is an intentional blurring of the surroundings around the main object of our attention. I'm sure you've seen a photograph in which a person is clear and sharp, and everything else in the background is blurred. This makes for a visually appealing photo because there's something pleasing to the physical eye about this technique, and it's pleasing to our mind's eye as well.

You can keep all of your desires in your awareness with soft focus and only hard focus on one thing until it becomes clear and manifests in your reality. The idea here is not to spread your attention too thin by trying to hard focus on multiple things at once. With that approach, it will take forever for things to manifest for you. Hard focus on one thing, and soft focus on everything else. When that one thing manifests, bring another one into hard focus, and so on.

The idea of soft focus is particularly useful when you have multiple desires that you want to see manifested. For instance, say you've always wanted to write a book. Go into your imagination and create what the cover looks like. Decide how many pages it will be and how it will be published. This is your hard focus. Start writing the book in your physical reality and stay hard focused on it until you have written the last word. Now, you still have other desires that you want to manifest, but during this time, they remain in soft focus.

Prioritize your desires so that you can have laser-focus energy to manifest the one that you would like to come first. You do not dismiss the other desires, instead you keep them in mind by using soft focus to hold them there.

Once the image becomes sharp and clear (manifests), then you've got it! Now, bring in another desire and make that one pop! This technique lets your mind stay at ease while creating your reality. Many times, we get all jumbled up because we are trying to manifest multiple desires at one time, and this causes stress, and we begin to question ourselves like, "Did I do it right?" or "Did I spend enough time on it?" or "Can I even manifest?"

It's important that we practice using our imagination, bringing things in and out of focus, from hard to soft, blurry to clear. However, it's just like anything else in life; it requires practice to excel. Be patient and have compassion for yourself. Don't get discouraged if it's difficult at first to see clear images in your mind. You *will* get better at it, and the beautiful thing is, it costs you nothing. You can practice this anytime, anywhere, and I promise you that if you commit to practicing using your imagination daily, you will achieve results. Be kind to yourself, and remember to have fun with this!

Many of us start something and never finish it because we get distracted and lose focus. I would imagine that if you look back on your life, you can see times when you were focusing on too many different things at once, and then you lost interest (focus), and they never came to pass. This doesn't mean that you're a failure. It's simply a matter of not keeping your focus on one thing.

Focusing on one thing at a time keeps us from becoming overwhelmed. As my dad used to say, "Inch by inch, everything's a cinch." There's no sense in biting off more than we can chew, and by keeping things in perspective, the manifestation of one desire often creates an umbrella effect, where our soft-focused desires begin to naturally appear in our reality. For example, you're hard-focused on getting that promotion at work, and it finally manifests. The extra money you are now making allows for your family to take that vacation that you had held in place with soft focus. See how this works?

Hold all your desires, dreams and goals in your awareness. They are safe there, and you've got them. No worries whatsoever. Now bring them in and out of focus, blurry to clear, soft to hard. You simply slide the focus meter up and down the scale because reality is negotiable.

SOFT FOCUS EXERCISE

Make a list of all your desires and prioritize them in order of importance to you. You need to be honest here. Don't feel guilty about having certain things take priority over others. This exercise requires you to be 100% authentic to get results. Take as much time as you need to make your list. Whatever the top item on your list is, make that your object of hard focus. Read your list every day to keep all your other desires in soft focus. You're not ignoring them. They're still in the picture. You're just blurring them so that your top item remains clear and sharp. Once this top desire manifests, do the same with your second item, and so on.

Read your list once every morning, once around lunchtime, and once right before bed. Keep this personal—it's for your eyes only. Before long, you're going to realize that everything on your list has come to pass, proving once again that life is negotiable.

"In the universe, there are things that are known, and things that are unknown, and in between there are doors."

- William Blake

CHAPTER 12
IN THE BODY OR OUT?

"I have said, Ye are Gods; and all of you are children of the most High" (Psalms 82:6-7). The "most High" is the universal formless consciousness, the source of all creation, and its "children" are the physical forms that the one consciousness is conceiving itself to be. We, as human beings, are both of these: formless consciousness and the physical forms it takes. We are God's children of the most high consciousness.

For each of us to properly negotiate reality as the God we are, we need to know as much about our divine nature as possible. While we are all well aware of the physical aspects of this, we also need to be aware of the metaphysical aspects of our divine nature because the two go hand in hand. We are multidimensional eternal beings having a temporary human experience.

"We are confident, I say, and willing rather to be absent from the body, and to be present with the Lord" (2 Cor. 5:8). This is one scripture that you're not going to hear the Church preach about too often, and even if you do,

I can almost guarantee that it will be taken out of context and misinterpreted.

What is this verse talking about? Like every other verse in the Bible, this particular verse is pointing to something deeper, something beyond the surface level of the words.

The Apostle Paul is speaking about "being absent from the body." Absence means leaving the body or not being present in the body. So, there must be something more to us, something that is able to leave the physical body. He then tells us that when we are absent from the body, we are present with the Lord. Intriguing, isn't it? I believe he is referring to our eternal spirit, our awareness, our God-self, and somehow, that part of us is able to leave our bodies. When we leave our bodies, we are in the unfiltered presence of our God-self.

One rainy afternoon in the fall of 1997, I decided to drive up to my local bookstore and browse through the spiritual section. They had all the usual fare, but as I scanned the shelves, something caught my eye: a book called *Out-of-Body Experiences: How to Have Them and What to Expect* by Robert Peterson. "Sounds interesting," I thought to myself. I grabbed the book, took it to the register and walked over to the cafe to grab a coffee before heading back to the house.

I didn't know much about out-of-body experiences or what to expect. Little did I know that was all about to change. Once I got home, I opened the curtains and looked at the view of downtown. It was still raining and overcast, and a low-level fog hung in the air around the buildings. The whole day seemed to have a rather strange vibe to it.

I sat down on the couch, noticing the house was quiet and calm. *A perfect day for a good book*, I thought and reclined back with a few pillows, took a sip of coffee, and opened the book to chapter one. I read all the way to the end of chapter two when suddenly I began to feel very tired, to the point where I was barely able to keep my eyes open. I laid the open book across my chest, reclined further back, and nodded off to sleep...or so I thought.

What happened next was something that changed my life forever. I didn't know it at the time, but my entire reality was about to shift. I began to feel deep internal and external vibrations that seemed to be coming from my innermost being. These were very strong, almost paralyzing, and they continued for several minutes. Then I began to hear very loud electrical sounds, like static, and this also seemed to be originating from inside me and seemed to be in sync with the vibrations. I was terrified. I actually thought I was dying.

The static sound grew louder and louder, eventually changing into a continuous electric hum. It was loud, intense, and overpowering. The vibrations also grew stronger, to the point where I didn't think I could take anymore, and then suddenly, there was a sound like velcro being ripped apart. It permeated my entire being, and then...*I was out*.

I had left my body. I was standing next to the couch watching myself sleep. Everything was as it was before. The open book was still resting on my chest. The house was quiet and calm. My coffee sat steaming on the end table. I was out of my physical body, but I was fully alert and aware of my surroundings. *I must have died*...the notion pierced my mind, the thought gripping me with fear. Suddenly, my awareness glanced back at the book on my chest, and I instantly made the connection. *I'm having an out-of-body experience*, I thought, and the fear began to subside. A sense of calmness swept over me in its place.

Confident that I hadn't died, I then walked over to the living room window and looked outside. The downtown buildings were still there, and everything was in its usual place; however, their appearance had changed. Now everything was outlined in a blue electric current, and the buildings themselves appeared less dense, almost translucent. It was actually beautiful to watch, and I felt an inner connectedness to everything, as if that electrical blue current was connecting me to everything I could see.

At this point, I found myself in another part of the house. I was now standing in my kitchen, staring at all the appliances. They too had the same electric blue current of energy outlining them. I looked at the kitchen counter and reached my hand out to touch it. When I did, my hand went right through it as if it wasn't there. Amazed at this, I tried again. Same thing. My hand went right through the countertop. It was no longer solid, and apparently neither was I.

I was in a state of complete wonder and wished that I could stay in this state forever. In that same moment that thought entered my mind, I was immediately "zapped" back into my physical body. I laid there for a few minutes, disoriented, trying to gather my thoughts about what had just happened.

I looked at the clock hanging on the living room wall and was shocked to see that only a few minutes had passed. Although the whole incident had only lasted a matter of minutes, it had felt like hours.

I thought about this experience often over the next few days, and when I did, I began to feel a new kind of confidence setting in. I wondered about the source of this confidence, and I slowly began to realize that I was no longer afraid of death. I now knew beyond a shadow of a doubt that we exist outside these physical bodies. I felt this immense sense of spaciousness. The place inside of me that the fear of death had occupied was now open and free. It felt really good. *"Oh death, where is thy sting? Oh grave, where is thy victory?"* (1 Cor. 15:55).

As mentioned earlier, this is not something that you're ever going to learn about in a traditional church; although, if you do, please send me the address. I want to go! Can you imagine what a fun church that would be? Fear mongers love fear, and they love to ask questions like, "If you died today, do you know where you'd go?" And while I can't answer that question indefinitely because I haven't "died," I do know that there's nothing to be afraid of. Someone once asked Ram Dass what he thought about death, and he just smiled and said, "Death is like taking off a tight shoe."

If you do a Google search on "out-of-body experience" or "astral projection," as it's sometimes called, you will get hundreds and hundreds of listings. You will also immediately learn that astral projection is a considerable threat to certain belief systems, just like meditation can be threatening.

The Bible says that when we are absent from the body, we are present with the Lord. This is speaking to the metaphysical aspect of our divine nature. God's presence is everywhere—it is our presence. Whether we are in the physical body or out of it, we are in God's presence. We can never get away from this presence because it is who we are. I believe that when we are out of the body, it is just a straight-up spiritual experience without the limitations of our physical senses.

The Bible speaks to us about astral projection on more than one occasion, and once again, the Apostle Paul gives us the lowdown on this. But first, you need to understand something about this particular Bible character. Paul was a humorist, and a lot of his writings conceal deep spiritual truths in a funny way. Unfortunately, most of his humor gets lost in translation.

It helps if you can think of what Paul's intention was in writing this way. I feel he was like the late great comedian George Carlin, who always said very important and relevant things in a joking manner. In the verse below, we see Paul describing his profound spiritual experience, but he's telling it as if it happened to a friend of his rather than himself. In a later verse, he says he was given "a thorn in the flesh" to keep him from bragging about this same experience. Paul was a bit of a rascal, and make no mistake about it, he's specifically speaking about himself in this verse. We suppose by telling it as if it happened to someone else, he's technically not bragging about it. Lol ...

Paul was sort of sneaky. He was funny. He was clever, and he was a mystic. One thing I have noticed about every great teacher, guru, or enlightened being I have encountered is that, without fail, there is something about them that just makes you scratch your head, raise an eyebrow, and snicker. I personally don't really trust anyone who claims to be enlightened if they act dead serious all the time; there's something that's cosmically funny about this world we live in, and truly enlightened people know this.

"I knew a man in Christ above fourteen years ago (whether in the body, I cannot tell; or whether out of the body, I cannot tell: God knoweth;) such an one caught up to the third heaven. And I knew such a man, (whether in the body, or out of the body, I cannot tell: God knoweth;) How that he was caught up to paradise, and heard unspeakable words, which it is not lawful for a man to utter. Of such an one will I glory, yet of myself I will not glory" (2 Cor. 12:2-5).

Here we have the Apostle Paul describing one of his many out-of-body experiences (OBE). He was a master at negotiating reality, and he knew full well the benefits of being able to leave the physical body. It seems to me that he had done it so often that he couldn't tell when he was in the body or out of it. Paul was aware of the multiple realities we exist in and that they blend in and out of one another, forming a type of hybrid universe of Self.

In this particular scenario, Paul left his body and ascended into what he called the "third heaven," where he heard such profound words that could not even be expressed with human language. It's a deeper inward hearing that only our spirit can know and understand. I'm sure you have experienced this at different times in your life, when you can't quite put your finger on it, but you know that you know that you know. This sort of "knowing" is very hard to describe to someone who hasn't had the same experience as you.

What is this "third heaven?" I think it's safe to say that he is speaking of another plane of existence, a different density where truth exists in its pure form and cannot be pressed through the filter of human language. It simply cannot be explained in a way that would make sense to someone here in three-dimensional density.

As you read through Paul's many writings, you will find that they are on another level compared to many other New Testament writers. All his writings are inspired by this "third level of heaven" experience he had, and this level can be experienced through astral projection. Paul would take these truths and sprinkle them throughout his books in the forms of allegories and stories, hoping that we could grasp them, thereby giving us an advantage in negotiating reality.

I personally believe that astral projection is something that every human being is capable of experiencing. There is an idea out there that we all leave our bodies every night when we go to sleep, and we're simply not aware of it when it happens. Awareness of something makes room for it in our lives. If you haven't known about OBEs until now, that's totally okay, because right here, right now, in this moment, you are expanding your awareness. Take a deep breath and relax into this new space you have created.

Love is the source and springboard of all out-of-body experiences, and *"there is no fear in love"* (1 John 4:18). This is important for you to understand as you explore your ability to leave your body. It can feel scary at first, and there is no way around that. It's a strange state of limbo which feels spooky and foreign, but also oddly familiar. Even though you may feel some initial fear at first, rest assured that your higher Self is right at home! It is a loving experience, a love so deep that our physical forms can't even understand it.

The desire to connect back to Source is a longing of your true Self, a "letting go" of physical reality to be closer to the One. I'm reminded of the old saying, "If you love something, set it free; if it returns to you, it's yours, and if it doesn't, it was never meant to be."

The good news is that your astral body always returns to your physical body during an OBE. It might sound odd, but we are actually attached by a never-ending silver cord that tethers our astral body to our physical body. This cord is mentioned in the book of Eccles. 12:6: *"Remember him, before the silver cord is severed, and the golden bow is broken, before the pitcher is shattered at the spring."*

The silver cord is your lifeline, and at the time of physical death, this cord is severed, at which point the spirit is free from the constraints of the body. You can put your mind at ease about this because astral projection can in no way cause this to happen. If anything, you're safer in your astral body because your spirit is free of any physical danger. It's similar to the idea that you are safer flying in an airplane than you are driving in a car.

One of the main benefits of having an OBE is losing the fear of death. You now know that you exist and are aware outside of your physical body, and this supplants a new perspective on life in your subconscious mind. You also know there are multiple planes of existence, one where things are dense and solid, like here on Earth, and others where things are subtle and non-visible to the waking eye.

Everything in life is made up of layers, even us! Have you ever met someone who looked big and scary, but then you found out they're just a big ol' teddy bear? Big and scary on one level, soft and sweet on another. We need to expand our awareness of life to make room for more life to come our way. We can do this by learning to look at everything in terms of layers. The next time you look at yourself in the mirror, realize that you consist of multiple layers. Even though you can't see them, you have layers. There are many aspects of your life that you may not even be aware of yet.

You are not just the one layer of your physical body. You are a multidimensional, multilayered spiritual being: the I AM. You are wearing a suit that allows you to explore this layer of organic life, and if you want, you can take that suit off and explore the many other layers of our reality. There is so much more than meets the eye.

Astral projection allows us to see that we resemble stage actors in a play wearing costumes. When we're not aware of this, it's easy to get caught up in the drama, especially when we think that this is all there is. Many people think life is only about what they can see, hear, taste, smell, and touch, but there is so much more happening behind the scenes. In Hinduism, they have a term for this: "Leela" which means "divine play." And, of course, we can't dismiss William Shakespeare's famous quote, "All the world's a stage, and all the men and women merely players. They have their exits and their entrances; And one man in his time plays many parts."

I don't want to go into great detail about all the OBEs I have experienced because I want yours to be fresh and uninfluenced by mine or any others. My goal is for you to become aware that you can do this if you choose. You certainly don't have to, but I personally feel like having this ability is an asset when it comes to negotiating reality. I believe that it is a natural ability that we are all born with. By simply becoming aware of this, we open the door between worlds.

Our reality is magical, filled with awe and wonder. The issue is that many of us no longer view it that way. We only see the same old stuff day after day, and we grow weary of it. But the truth is we came here for the magic! No one describes the magic of astral projection better than the pioneer of OBEs, Robert Monroe. In his books, he describes an interesting idea (and this is just an idea, so obviously no one can prove any of this) that the earth is almost like an amusement park, and at one point, we all stood anxiously in line for our chance to come here. He describes that before we entered these human forms, we were off exploring the various realms of existence and having wonderful adventures. He believes we were once very excited for our opportunity to experience humanity, because this is the realm of feeling and emotion which allows us to fully experience life on earth. Apparently, we waited a long time to get our ticket before we passed through the veil of forgetfulness, exited our mother's womb, and let out our first cry as a newborn human baby. This is definitely an intriguing perspective.

This whole human experience is all about the senses and feeling. So many of us run from our feelings, but this is the entire reason we are here—to feel. Emotions are not something to avoid, rather they are something to lean into since they are our guides. If we aim to live an intense life filled with many different experiences, we must understand that strong and intense emotions are part of the deal.

We are here for the experience, and astral projection helps us remember that. You are so much more than you think you are. Simply open yourself to this concept, try to be objective and don't just dismiss it out of hand because it may be something that you don't know about. You have the mind of Christ, so be open to everything and attached to nothing. If you make the conscious decision to experience astral projection, your entire reality will expand beyond measure, and you will come into the flow of life in a new way having one awesome experience after another.

There are many astral projection techniques, and several books are available that detail the subject. I have read and researched a majority of them. I must tell you, though, most of them tend to make it more complicated than it needs to be. What works for someone else may or may not work for you, and that's okay. What I know to be true, based on personal experience, is that by simply holding the idea of astral projection in your mind, your awareness of it will open the door to the experience itself.

The best technique is not actually a technique at all. Simply become aware that your astral body is residing inside your physical body, and as you go about your day, imagine your astral body doing the same movements as your physical body. For instance, when you open a door, imagine your astral hand opening the door. Your astral body is doing everything your physical body is doing, just under the skin. Think of your physical body as a glove that your astral body is wearing. The more you practice this, the more natural it will become, and before long, you will begin to feel the presence of your astral body vibrating from within.

You can practice sensing your astral body at any time and any place. When you are sitting still in meditation, try to sense your astral body also sitting within. You can also imagine your astral body lifting up and out of your physical body. Sometimes being aware of this one thing alone is enough to induce an OBE.

Another beneficial time to sense your astral body is during the hypnagogic state, also referred to as State Akin to Sleep or S.A.T.S. We all enter this state at least twice a day, once when we first wake up and once right before we fall asleep. The idea here is that the subconscious mind is very impressionable during these times, and if you impress it with the intention to leave your body, it accepts it as truth and produces the experience. You can play around with this state, but try not to let yourself fall asleep...and watch all the crazy images and sounds that dance around in your mind. It's actually a lot of fun and something you can look forward to every evening.

Another simple method is best used right before a nap. Fully relax and absorb yourself in the silence. As you do this, you may hear a slight hum or subtle ringing in your ears. Magnify this sound by focusing your attention on it. Try to trace the source of the sound, as this can lead you into the vibrational state, which is the beginning of an OBE.

When we are out of our bodies, we are who we were before we entered this human incarnation. We can clearly see that our physical bodies are nothing more than a suit of senses that hold our eternal spirits, which allow us to experience the world around us in a sensual way, like a deep-sea diver who puts on a scuba suit and oxygen tanks to explore the depths of the ocean. Your human body is simply a suit that allows you to explore the world of humanity.

"I was in the spirit on the Lord's Day, and heard behind me a great voice, as of a trumpet, Saying, I am Alpha and Omega, the first and the last..." (Revelation 1:10-11). Here we have an example of astral projection from the life of John. He was "in the spirit" and out of his body, and in this state, he hears the voice of God. When we are out of our body, we are in our spirit form, and it is much easier in this form to hear the voice of our higher

Self (God, I AM) because it is not muffled by our flesh and bodily senses. When you are "in the spirit," you have no doubt who you truly are. When the play of life gets overwhelming, OBEs are a wonderful reminder that nothing is really as it seems.

With all that being said, all you need to do is hold the idea of being able to have an OBE in your awareness. Practice being aware of your astral body inside you, and set your intention to be that of John, to hear the voice of God. This is an uncomplicated way to commune with your higher Self and possibly induce an out-of-body experience.

Astral projection is something that comes naturally to us as human beings. It will happen organically for you if you simply hold it in your awareness and allow it to be. You don't have to try and figure it all out because your higher Self knows exactly what to do and how to do it. All things are working together for your good, and you will experience being out of your body when it is right for you. No worries!

ASTRAL AWARENESS BREATHING EXERCISE

Duration: 20 min

This exercise can be used to expand your awareness of your astral body. The pineal gland, located in the middle of your brain, is the headquarters of your mystical experiences. Stimulating this gland will automatically expand your awareness of your astral Self. We can promote this part of the brain through breathing.

Sit with your legs crossed and clench your sphincter muscle (sounds weird, but it works). Now, suck in your abdomen muscles, and draw in a deep, slow breath in through the nose. Visualize and feel this breath running up the base of your spine and into the pineal gland in the center of your brain. Hold the breath right in this spot for as long as you can, and then exhale slowly. Repeat this breath as many times as you can. You can practice this any time, but for whatever odd reason, 4 a.m. seems to have an intensifying effect, enhancing your ability to feel the energy swirling around you. It will take a little practice to get into the flow of this breath, but after a short time, it will become routine. Keep at it. Consistent practice is key for this one, and before long a mystical experience will be yours!

"Father of father, what do we here, in the land of unbelief and fear? The land of dreams is better far, above the light of the morning star."

- William Blake

CHAPTER 13
DREAMS AND VISIONS

"And it shall come to pass afterward, that I will pour out my spirit upon all flesh, and your sons and daughters shall prophesy, your old men shall dream dreams, and your young men shall see visions" (Joel 2:28).

One way our higher Self communicates its wisdom to us is through dreams and visions. The spirit of God—as it is referred to in the Bible—is, in fact, your higher Self. The verse above explains that it has been poured out upon all of us. In other words, we all have a higher Self. This is the divine part of our nature, and it knows everything we need to know to negotiate reality.

Our higher Self speaks to us continually throughout our human incarnations. Sometimes, It is in a still, small voice that we can hear only when we are quiet, in the depths of meditation. Other times, It speaks to us in dreams when our conscious mind is asleep. This is especially beneficial for us in today's world, where most people are so consumed with the hustle and bustle of daily life that they rarely make the time to quiet their minds. Our higher Self has got our back and is an ever-present ally always in our corner. It knows us inside and out, and It doesn't get Its feelings hurt when we are too busy to acknowledge It. It will simply wait until we fall asleep to give us Its guidance. In this state, we can offer no resistance to its instruction.

"In a dream, in a vision of the night, when deep sleep falleth upon men, in slumberings upon the bed; Then he openeth the ears of men, and sealeth their instruction" (Job 33:15-16). This verse gives us the reason and purpose of dreams. They are a time when we receive instructions from God (our higher Self). Now, I think we can safely say that not all dreams are this way, but sometimes they are, and we need to be mindful of this.

I'm certain that you have had one of these dreams in which you have received instruction from your higher Self. These types of dreams generally leave an impression on you, and you can feel them in the core of your being upon waking. Sometimes, you can't quite put your finger on it, but you know that it was different because there was a vividness to it, and it sticks with you for a few days, weeks, or even a lifetime. These "higher dreams" serve as guideposts for us, roadmarks along our spiritual path.

When we experience these "higher dreams," often they are in the form of a scene, like a movie in which we are the main character. These dreams are commonly symbolic and contain elements that require us to dig a little deeper to see their significance. Not unlike the Bible itself, these dreams should not be taken at face value. There is something deeper in these dreams that our higher Self is communicating to us that requires our interpretation.

Another way in which God (our higher Self) speaks to us is in the form of recurring dreams. We may have the same dream two nights in a row, or we may have the same dream a year later. In some cases, we may have the same dream repeatedly throughout our lives. Recurring dreams reveal to us certain beliefs that we have embedded in our subconscious mind, beliefs that no longer serve us, or beliefs we may not even be aware of. Our higher Self reveals them to us so we can acknowledge them, learn from them, and then eliminate them from our lives.

Let me give you an example of a recurring dream I experienced. I had this same dream, or a variation of it, for years. I kept having it until I took the time to acknowledge it and receive its instruction. In this dream, everything always started out fine. My family and I would be sitting in the living room or driving in a car, going about our normal day, nothing extraordinary. Then I would look out the window, either from the living room or the car, and see a tornado off in the distance. It would either be just forming and dropping down out of the sky, or it would be on the ground wreaking havoc. It was always off in the distance. Sometimes, there would be multiple tornados that would be on the ground at once. Some of them were large, and some small.

During these dreams, I always felt a sense of urgency, fear, and lack of control. I felt like the only thing I could do to keep my family safe was to run away because, in these dreams, the tornados were always heading our way, and just as we would be trying to escape the impending doom, I would wake up.

These dreams were frightening. I often woke up breathing heavily with my heart racing, and it would take me at least an hour to recover. Eventually, the feeling would fade, and things return to normal.

I can't count how many times I've had this dream over the years, but it was so often that I started to have this sense of "here we go again" when the dream would start. Nothing too terrible ever happened in the dream.

The tornados would never actually reach my family and me, but I knew they were coming toward us and the damage they were capable of doing.

This recurring dream continued for the span of fifteen years until one day, when I finally took the time to acknowledge that maybe there was a message here. I began to meditate on its significance. Damn, we humans can be so hard-headed sometimes. It took me fifteen years to acknowledge that my higher Self was doing Its best to communicate with me! The instructions from this dream changed my life—and that could have happened much earlier if I had just slowed down and listened!

As I began to meditate on the dream, my beliefs and fears began to rise to the surface. I discovered that these tornados represented false beliefs and fears that I had buried deep in my subconscious mind: fear of the future, fear of a lack of control over reality, fear that life was happening to me and that there was nothing I could do about it except maybe run away. I realized that, due to certain experiences in my past, I had formed a false belief that the world couldn't be trusted and that something bad was always about to happen. I had also formed a belief about myself that I would never be "good enough" or amount to anything and that I would always be running from reality.

I went deep into this. I won't give all the nitty gritty details, but I know that many of my false beliefs were implanted in me while growing up in churches that taught us to fear God. Things like hell, a lake of fire, Satan, demons, the great tribulation, the rapture, and of course, the pièce de résistance—the great white throne of judgment day. These concepts are so damaging to a young mind! I lived with this subconscious fear for years, and it kept me from enjoying my life.

As I began to acknowledge and eliminate these embedded false beliefs, something significant happened. I had one final dream about a tornado—

but this one was different. I was standing alone in a field, and I could see for miles in all directions. It was a beautiful summer day, with blue skies and the sun shining warm and bright. Then, a giant tornado dropped right out of the sky directly in front of me. It was much larger than any from my previous dreams, and something was different about it. It hovered and spun violently just a few feet from where I stood, but I wasn't afraid, I wasn't panicked, and I didn't try to run. At this moment, I heard a voice speak from inside of it. The tornado itself spoke and asked me a question, "Do you want me to leave, or do you want me to stay?" "I want you to leave," I said. The moment the words left my lips, the tornado evaporated without leaving a trace.

When I woke up from this dream, I knew that I was free. I could feel it. Something in my consciousness had shifted. All that space the embedded fears and false beliefs occupied in my life was now freed up. It was like a breath of fresh air! I felt lighter. I felt a sense of relief. A weight had been lifted off my shoulders, and I've never had another dream about a tornado since. I finally got the message and received the instruction.

Dreams will always be personal and individualized when they contain instructions from your higher Self, but as mentioned earlier, not all dreams are going to be like this. Some dreams will be random brain dumps. These are the ones that make no sense whatsoever, and there is no rhyme or reason for them. It's like emptying the recycling bin on your computer. Your higher Self is just trying to eliminate insignificant junk mail from your hard drive. Discernment is needed to know which dreams are just trash and which carry guidance or messages from your higher Self.

So, what is a vision, and is it the same as a dream? While dreams and visions share similar qualities, there is a difference between the two. We experience dreams when our conscious mind is asleep, and we experience visions while we are fully awake and conscious. A vision is most often a foretelling of future events and presents an outline or framework for our life (and in some cases, the life of another). Just like a dream, they will hold symbolism and require thoughtful interpretation if we're going to rely on them to negotiate reality.

Visions generally don't happen as frequently as dreams, and while some people are "gifted" and do experience frequent visions, most of us only experience one in our entire lifetime. A regular meditation or prayer practice seems to increase the chance of receiving a vision for our life. When we ascend in consciousness through these practices, it allows for us to see things that we wouldn't normally see.

"Call unto me [consciousness], and I will answer thee, and shew thee great and mighty things, which thou knowest not" (Jeremiah 33:3).

When we launch out into the deep, infinite waters of our consciousness through regular prayer and meditation, we are told in this verse that we will be shown great and mighty things of which we are unaware. This describes what a vision is, and when we experience this, it's like the curtain of life opens up and we are shown the metaphysical framework of our physical reality.

I have personally had only one vision in my life so far, and I've pondered it for years. Only recently have I discovered its meaning. But even though I didn't understand it at the time, it served as a spiritual lighthouse, a beacon to look toward that seemed to contain my purpose in life. We all have a purpose, a reason we are here, and a vision can solidify that understanding for us. I want to share my one vision with you because perhaps you have experienced something similar, and since we all share the same universal consciousness, it may help you interpret what you've seen.

One afternoon in the late 90s, I was in college at the University of New Mexico. It had been a particularly stressful day, and I was spending some time in deep meditation and Bible study. I was exhausted. I laid my head down on the table, not to sleep but to rest for a minute or two. When I did, my consciousness shifted, and suddenly, I became aware that I was running through a large desert area with a great war going on all around me.

As I ran through the middle of this war, awareness prickled of another person at my side, locked arm in arm with me. This other wore a hooded cloak, and although I couldn't see his face, I somehow knew that it was Jesus. This war was vast, stretching as far as the eye could see, and we were running through the middle of it completely unphased and unafraid.

Looking ahead, I could see a large wooden building, and it became apparent that this is where we were headed. We continued to run through this war without anyone ever noticing us. Eventually we arrived at the giant wooden structure. We opened the front door and stepped inside.

This mammoth structure was filled with windows that looked out in all directions. I could see the battle continuing around us. There was a huge crowd in the main room of this building, thousands of people, young and old, of all nationalities, and they were all happy, laughing and having a great time without any worry about what was happening just outside. There was a very tangible sense of peace and calm inside this space. I stood there observing this, still locked arm in arm with this cloaked individual at my side. We then began to ascend a massive spiral staircase that led to the very top of the building. Walking arm and arm up each step, we arrived at a large platform that resembled a diving board that looked out over the crowd of people below. We walked out onto this plank, and when we reached the edge, the being at my side evaporated. He was gone in the blink of an eye, and then I heard a thunderous voice that seemed to come from deep within me and also beyond, everywhere all at once. I instinctively knew this was the voice of God, consciousness itself, and it said, "You are the captain of the ship." This startled me back to reality, and the whole scene disappeared as quickly as it had come.

I carried that vision with me for over twenty-five years. I sought out very prominent religious leaders in hopes that they could interpret it for me. I asked friends and family, and while some of them made some good guesses, nothing they said resonated with me as the truth—and then I came across Neville Goddard.

In lectures from the late 60s and early 70s, Goddard talked about an experience he had that he referred to as "The Promise." I'm not going to try to describe his personal experience, because there's no way I could do it justice. In essence, the idea he shares is that everyone at some point in their life will have a vision in which they no longer see God as anything other than themselves. They will experience God as their Self, one being, no separation.

Twenty-five years later, I was finally able to interpret my vision. All this time, I didn't know what the thing meant. Captain of the ship? The war? The building? The spiral staircase? The cloaked figure at my side? Even though I didn't know its meaning, I knew it was significant and could sense a purpose in it that kept me searching, giving me a reason to go even deeper into consciousness over the years.

At the beginning of the vision, I was running arm in arm with Jesus across a vast desert with war erupting on all sides of us. I couldn't see his face, but I knew it was him. We were side-by-side. Two separate people. Seeing Jesus this way, separate from ourselves, is like running through a battlefield where reality is very hard to negotiate. It's an unstable way to live, both mentally and physically. Reality will always appear chaotic when we see Jesus as a separate entity.

The war zone I was running through represented my outside physical reality, and the large wooden structure represented the internal reality where everything was peaceful, happy, joyful, humorous, and safe, regardless of what was going on outside.

The spiral staircase represents the human spine which travels upward to the mind. I ascended the staircase and walked out onto a platform (the mind) and suddenly, the being at my side disappeared. I no longer saw him, and in that moment, I heard the voice of God thundering from within myself. "You are the captain of the ship." The ship is our human life, and we are the captain of it. No one else, no outside separate God, just you, just me, we. We are the captains of our ships.

When we rise in consciousness and no longer see God as separate from ourselves, an internal happiness and contentment emerges. At this point we can start to be the captains of our lives, and we can steer them in any direction we choose. We no longer rely on an outside source for direction. We no longer have to wonder and worry about what God's will is for our lives; we are God, and our will be done.

It's unfortunate, but many people are relying on an external God to be the captain of their ship. They wonder why they're not truly happy, viewing life as nothing but a struggle and eventually concluding that this must be God's will for their lives. That's a completely unnecessary way to live. We all go through some tough times; that's part of the deal, but it's not intended to be a way of life. A miserable existence is not God's will. If you don't want to live that way, if it's not your will, then it's not God's either. You are one and the same.

I wholeheartedly believe, along with Goddard, that everyone will have this experience of God. It will be different for each of us, simply because we are all different people, but it will happen at some point in one's life. Maybe tonight, maybe tomorrow, maybe ten years from now, or in another space and time, but everyone will experience God as themselves. It has to be this way because we are all one. At some point, we will all be drawn back into the One Being that we are. No one knows when it will happen, but like a thief in the night, the day of the Lord will come, and you will see the Lord as none other than yourself.

Dreams and visions play such a huge part in our lives, yet they don't seem to get much attention. The average person spends over 200,000 hours of their lives sleeping. That's one-third of our life, and 25% of that time is spent dreaming. This means that we spend roughly six years of our life in dreamland! So, yeah, I'd say it's important.

It's no wonder that we have sayings like "living the dream" and "dream big" or "in your dreams." These common phrases give us clues to the dreamlike nature of what we call "reality." Because, as above, so below. What if we really are "living the dream?" I think there's a pretty good chance that we are.

"In the beginning was the word, and the word was with God, and the word was God." (John 1:1)

"And the Word was made flesh..." (John 1:14)
So, let's go back to the very beginning.

"And God said, let us make man in our own image, after our likeness" (Genesis 1:26).

This is the Word, or God (consciousness) becoming flesh as a human being. This human being was called Adam. God (consciousness) became a human being.

"And the Lord caused a deep sleep to fall upon Adam, and he slept ..." (Genesis 2:21).

The Bible doesn't ever mention that Adam (God in the flesh) woke up from his sleep. Is it possible that God is dreaming all of this from beginning to end, and we are living inside that dream? The Bible says of God, *"I am the Alpha and the Omega, the beginning and the end, the first and the last"* (Revelation 22:13).

The Bible is a psychological drama that takes place and unfolds in the consciousness of human beings, and since consciousness is the only reality, the I AM is the first human and the last human, it's the beginning and the end and everything in between. Could it be that everything in between is God's dream, our dream, and we dream within that dream?

Dreams are like alternate realities in which we exist simultaneously with what we call our physical waking reality. There are worlds within worlds, and we should pay attention and become aware of these alternate realities that we visit every night. As we do this, we can start to see that our physical reality is a metaphysical blending of these various dimensions in which we coexist.

Information in the dream reality is useful here in this reality and vice versa. This is a great part of what makes life so magical, and it's unfortunate that it often gets overlooked. Your daytime reality can be a lot more fun by simply bringing more awareness to your nighttime reality. You get to go on an all-expense-paid vacation to Wonderland every single night of your life. Enjoy it, learn from it, and you will see that reality is indeed negotiable.

A good practice is to start writing down your dreams. Keep a notebook or journal next to your bed at night, and as soon as you wake up in the morning, record your dreams. If you can't remember them all the time, no worries. You can easily change this by setting an intention to remember before you drift off to sleep. Simply intend to remember your dreams, and don't sweat it if it takes a little time. The more awareness you bring to your dreams, the easier they will be to recall. It will happen. Just be patient with yourself, and before you know it, you will be remembering your dreams on a regular basis.

Once you start recalling your nighttime adventures and writing them down, look over them from time to time, and you may start to see patterns emerging. These patterns will be messages from your higher Self that can help you negotiate reality.

Have you ever had a dream so intense that you could feel it in your physical body upon awakening? Perhaps it was a scary dream, and you could feel that fear, or perhaps it was a sexual dream, and you awoke in a state of arousal. This shows you the blending of the multiple realities where we coexist. The dream reality caused an effect on your physical body in this reality.

Experiment with this and have fun with it! Don't be afraid of your dreams. There is a part of you that is completely at home there. You're a local, and you have every right to be there and explore as much as you want. Remind yourself throughout the day that you are a dreamer and intend to remember your dreams.

As you practice this, you will start to edge closer to lucid dreaming. Lucid dreaming is when you become aware from inside a dream that you are dreaming, and when this happens, you will be able to control your dream and create whatever you want. This can be a lot of fun, and the more you do this, the more you will clearly see that you are the creator of your reality, and you may even realize that you are lucid dreaming right now.

BLEED THROUGH – DREAM AWARENESS EXERCISE

This exercise takes advantage of the fact that what we do in our waking reality has an effect on our dream reality and vice versa. There is a "bleed through" effect that happens between these two worlds when we become aware that we are existing in multiple realities at the same time. This is a very powerful yet simple method for triggering a lucid dream.

Ask yourself, "Am I dreaming?" Now, add a visual aid to that. For instance, whenever you open a door, ask yourself, "Am I dreaming?" Or maybe every time you look at your watch, your phone, or a clock on the wall, ask yourself out loud, "Am I dreaming?"

Practice doing this for a week straight in your normal everyday waking life, and one night, while you're dreaming, you will look at your phone, a clock, your watch, or open a door, and your dream self will ask, "Am I dreaming?" This will trigger you to wake up inside your dream. At this point, you are lucid, and you can control this dream reality in any way that you want.

Consistency is key with this exercise, and if this is something you're interested in pursuing, be dedicated in asking yourself, "Am I dreaming?" and set your intention every night to lucid dream and to remember these dreams, too. Before long, you will realize that you are the captain of the ship in that reality as well as this one.

"No bird soars too high if he soars with his own wings."

- William Blake

CHAPTER 14
THE HOTSPOT AND THE CLOUD

I'm sure you've heard the phrase "go with the flow." If you've spent any time lately in the spiritual or self-help space, you've also probably heard discussions on "flow states." Flow states are states of being where everything flows for you and through you. It's a time when things are working out, and you're accomplishing so much. Creativity is flowing, momentum is on your side, and it's moving you forward and through what you want to do.

We want to be in the flow, but what is "the flow?" The flow is the forward motion of the universe's positive energy, like an ocean current or a river. If you stand on the bank and drop a leaf into the water, it will travel along effortlessly because of the natural flow of the current. The leaf is not trying to swim downstream—it is simply in the flow and can travel a great distance just by being. The universal flow of positive energy is something that we can all drop into any time we desire, simply through our intention to do so.

As above, so below. As we talk about getting in the flow, it's essential to realize that our physical reality is a lower representation of the higher spiritual reality, and the things we use every day in this 3D reality are often copies of their spiritual counterpart. That said, let's talk about the hotspot and the cloud. You can drop yourself into the flow by mentally connecting directly to that positive current via your own personal hotspot.

The universal flow is like Wi-Fi. The only problem is that many of us are disconnected. Think about your cell phone. You can do a few things on it without Wi-Fi, but you're fairly limited. However, once you are connected, your phone becomes nearly unlimited in its capabilities. And so it is with us: we need to be connected.

Many people struggle to accomplish things because they are disconnected from the universal flow. They rely on their effort to make things happen instead of allowing the flow to carry them along.

It's not too hard to get in the flow. It's as simple as connecting your phone to Wi-Fi. Imagine that you are pulling up to Starbucks, your phone automatically detects their Wi-Fi signal, and all you have to do is click "connect," and then you're on. Our higher Self is always in the universal flow; however, our lower self needs to connect, and we can do this no matter where we are by utilizing our own personal "hotspot," just like you would do on your phone.

Every single one of us has a personal hotspot. The Hindus call it the "Atman," the Christians call it the "Holy Spirit," others call it the "God Spark," and we call it the "hotspot." The hotspot is the magical god particle hidden inside you. Imagine it as a little flame that sits right inside your consciousness, allowing you unlimited access to the universal flow that can be used anytime and anywhere.

You can activate your hotspot by becoming still and placing your awareness in the center of your brain, where your pineal gland is located. Quiet your mind for a moment or two, breathe in slowly, exhale slowly, and imagine a flame growing bigger as if you were blowing on a dimly lit campfire until it ignites. You have turned on your hotspot and will feel the mental sensation of connecting to the universal flow.

This does not need to be a long, drawn-out process. It takes merely a moment or two when you have the intention to connect. You can do this during meditation sessions, but you can also do it in your car, in the bathroom, at the grocery store, or even at work. It's wonderful if you can do this every night before you go to sleep and every morning before you leave the house.

When you connect to the flow via your personal hotspot, you will have unlimited access to the universe's positive energy throughout your day. Use this every time you feel disconnected or when you start to feel anxious or stressed out; take a moment to turn on your hotspot, reconnect, and drop back into the flow. It's very simple, but like many things in life, it has become overly complicated by those who have tried to turn it into some kind of dogmatic exercise that must be followed to the letter.

Simply set your intention to connect to the flow because your intention carries more weight than you think. Calm yourself, and place your awareness in the center of your mind. Hang out here for a moment with your intention to connect, and in a few moments, you will be connected. You may experience resistance for a minute or two if you're having a particularly stressful day. Don't sweat it, you'll connect, and when you do, you will sense a feeling of oneness with all others who are connected at that time.

You will gain access to the Cloud when you use your hotspot to drop into the flow. As above, so below. In our modern physical reality, the Cloud is where all our digital information is stored, and in our spiritual reality, it works in a similar fashion. The Cloud is often referred to as the Akashic records, or simply "Akash." The Akashic records (or Cloud) are said to be an infinite cosmic library where all our thoughts, feelings, wisdom, knowledge, and experiences are stored, and as such, they are manifestations of the collective higher Self of humanity. As above, so below.

"Dost thou know the balancings of the clouds, the wondrous works of him which is perfect in knowledge?" (Job 37:16). The "balancings of the clouds" is associated with perfect knowledge, and perfect knowledge is the heart of our universe. We should always aim to live from our hearts, speak from our hearts, and follow our hearts. The heart is where our deepest desires reside. When we access the Cloud, our hearts are opened to the knowledge of the universe, which we can use to negotiate reality.

During the process of writing this book, I accessed the Cloud one morning as I was awakening from sleep. I was in a hypnagogic state (half awake/half asleep), and I observed a cloud hovering in the room just above my bed. It was honestly the most beautiful thing I have ever seen. The atmosphere around it was filled with unspeakable joy and clean, positive energy that was billowing and expanding with a supernatural fluid-like motion.

Coming out of the center of the cloud were the most exotic colors in the universe, colors that we don't even have names for in this physical reality. They expanded and formed themselves into all different shapes and sizes. I intuitively knew that this exquisite beauty was creation itself, forever in our midst and that it is available to us at any time.

Awareness of the Cloud has a very palpable effect on our lives and is especially beneficial for us when we need perfect knowledge. For example, when you are discussing an important and rather emotional issue with your friends or family, use your imagination and see this beautiful Cloud in your mind's eye. Be aware that it is in your midst. Your awareness will allow people to open up and speak the truth from their heart. Even an uncomfortable and difficult conversation can result in something beautiful.

"For thy mercy is great unto the heavens, and thy truth unto the clouds" (Psalms 57:10). When you need to tap into the heart of a matter, the truth, the Cloud opens the heart and allows its loving energy to flow. The Cloud can bring intense emotions out into the open, but this is a positive event because the truth leads you and others to the perfect knowledge of the issue at hand. It is like a gentle yet firm coaxing energy that breaks through the mental barriers and facades we have built up around ourselves. Think of it like a beautiful flower growing up through a concrete sidewalk. There is so much beauty and so much truth that no amount of hardness can prevent it from blooming.

It's ironic that we use a phrase like "he's got his head in the clouds" as an insult when, in essence, this is exactly where our heads should be. We can be "down to earth" and have our "head in the clouds" at the same time. It is a magical, empowering, and heartfelt way to live.

We can make our lives as magical or non-magical as we wish. There is no right or wrong way. Life just "is," and all we have to do is just "be." Always be yourself. The world needs your authenticity.

"And the Lord went before them by day in a pillar of a cloud, to lead them the way..." (Exodus 13:21).

The universe and all it contains is simply yourself pushed out onto the screen of space, so why not push out some magic? Why not push out some happiness? This is how all of reality is created. We live in a world where there is so much more than meets the eye, and the Cloud can help lead us to the perfect knowledge of these things unseen.

The magic of life is all around us. The problem is that our connection to it was lost somewhere along the way. Sometimes, this happens due to an undesired reality imposed on us when we were young—a paradoxical environment that pickpockets our magic and yet remains unmagical itself.

As time goes on we tend to get used to this manner of reality, and it seems the magic of life is lost. And while it may, in fact, be lost, it is not gone. You are the universe, you are all of creation, and you are God playing all the parts. You have the magic in you. It may have been gestating for a long time, but it's never too late! Find it inside you. I assure you it's there, in the core of your being. Use your hotspot to feel your connection to it, and push!

CLOUD CONNECTION EXERCISE

Sit quietly and breathe in and out through the nose slowly and deeply until you feel your body and mind relaxing. On your last exhale, let it out with a long sigh. Continue to breathe as normal. Place your awareness in the center of your head and imagine you are breathing into that spot. Visualize a small flame in the area of your pineal gland that glows stronger and brighter with each breath. Sense your connection to the universal consciousness and relax into that connection. You are safe here. Now imagine a beautiful cloud billowing all around you. Whatever colors you see are the perfect colors of creation. Repeat the following mantra either aloud or to yourself, "I am one with myself and the universe." Continue with the mantra until you feel yourself absorbed into the oneness. At this point, allow the mantra to recede and sit quietly for a few minutes, basking in the glow of your connection to the source of perfect knowledge. Slowly, very slowly, open your eyes.

"I must create a system or be enslaved by another mans; I will not reason and compare, my business is to create."

- William Blake

CHAPTER 15

IMPOSTER SYNDROME

Throughout this book, we have learned that consciousness is the only reality and that our creative imagination is the way to manifest our desires within that reality. Our imagination is the Christ of scripture. We are God in the flesh. We are the creators of our life experiences, and if we are to have a good experience, we must also learn to coexist not only with one another but with the limitations of being in these human bodies.

On the previous page, there is a quote by William Blake. He says in this quote that if we are not intentionally using our imagination to create our personal reality, then we can easily become enslaved to other people's belief systems. It is unlikely that we have intentionally used our imagination to create reality for our entire lives. Because of this, an unfortunate and undetected mindset may have become embedded into our subconscious minds. These "other" beliefs are projected outward into our physical reality through our speech and actions. If left unchecked, they develop into routine behavior, which gives birth to an identity called the ego.

Our greatest limitation as humans is the ego. There are a plethora of books and videos available on this subject, so we won't do a deep dive into all the different expressions and attributes of the ego. What we aim to do is expose the one aspect of the ego that hinders us the most while negotiating reality—and then, once exposed, how to use it for our benefit.

The ego is not our enemy, and it's not necessarily our friend either; it just is. It's more like a pretend identity, a facade that serves as a defense mechanism for us. One aspect of this constructed identity that seems to hinder us more than any other is the phenomenon of the poverty mindset.

If you feel guilty when you wish for more than you currently have, if you find yourself limiting your abundance because it feels like "too much" or "unfair," if you feel shame for having while others have not, if you hold on tightly to your money or if you secretly have disdain for those who seem to have it all together, then you likely have a poverty or "lack" mindset attached to your ego.

This is a tricky one because it doesn't just show up one day introducing itself on our doorstep saying, "Hi! I'm the poverty mindset you ordered!" No, it trickles in very slowly and subtly through our life experiences starting at a very early age. This can and often does come from what we hear in church, what we hear our parents talking about, and what we see in movies and on TV.

Let's think about this: If you grew up in a fundamental Christian Church, you were probably taught that humans are simply hopeless sinners and that if it wasn't for Jesus dying for our sins, we'd all end up burning in hell. You were probably taught that poverty is a virtue, that Jesus and his disciples were poor, and that the poor widow woman who gave her last two mites in the offering is someone to be admired (Luke 21:1-4). These Bible stories get misinterpreted by those who are teaching them to the point where we learn at a very early age that being poor is a necessary part of following Jesus. On the other hand, if you grew up in a megachurch or have spent a lot of time attending one, you were probably under the impression that if you were really serving God, you would have a gold-plated personal jet parked in your driveway. Neither of these depictions are accurate. It's no wonder people are so confused about prosperity.

But it's not just the Church that causes this confusion—it's our life experiences. Growing up, I felt my parents were always struggling with money. Sometimes we seemed to have more than enough and sometimes we ate cereal with water. Listening to my parents talk about their struggles, I started to develop an idea that the world was a tough place and that we were lucky just to get by. These were the seeds being planted that the ego would eventually cultivate into a poverty mindset.

This mindset stuck with me and developed into a full-blown mentality as I grew up. As a result, I rarely experienced a truly abundant life. It wasn't until I began to renew my mind (doing away with unhealthy thought patterns and replacing them with truth) that my reality began to change. It wasn't overnight. It was a process. It takes time to unwire old belief systems, especially when it comes to the poverty mentality.

Not only can a poverty mindset keep us from receiving abundance, but it can also cause feelings of guilt when we do attract abundance into our lives. It can cause us to feel ashamed that we are doing better than others, as if we've done something wrong by bettering ourselves. This is insane thinking, but it's very common, and it's all because of the ego's defense system. There is nothing wrong with living an abundant life — it's one of the main reasons we're here. *"The thief cometh not but to steal and to kill and to destroy. I am come that they may have life, and that they may have it more abundantly"* (John 10:10).

The "thief" is the poverty mentality, which steals your joy, kills your happiness, and destroys your creative energy. The purpose of Jesus (our creative imagination) is for us to create an abundant life for ourselves and others. It might mean never-ending riches, the jet in the driveway, time to rest, the space to create, a healthy body, or an abundance of friends. Whatever you can imagine, the process is the same.

Jesus (imagination) was given to everybody by grace, and grace simply means undeserved, unearned favor. *"For by grace are ye saved through faith; and that not of yourselves: it is the gift of God. Not of works, lest any man should boast"* (Ephesians 2:8-9).

Every one of us has been given an imagination. *"For God so loved the world, that he gave his only begotten son [Jesus/Imagination] that whosoever believeth in him shall not perish, but have everlasting life"* (John 3:16, paraphrased). Again, the purpose of having an imagination is so that we can live an abundant life.

Since this wonderful imagination was given to all of us—the key word here being given—it stands to reason that we didn't earn it, and we didn't do anything to deserve it. So when we create abundance with it (which is what it's for), we need not feel unworthy, guilty, or ashamed. As a matter of fact, it is exactly the opposite. Let's tell the world the good news that imagination creates reality. It's for everyone, everywhere, regardless of race, age, gender, class. This is the true gospel, the good news!

False beliefs do not serve us in any way, but the world is full of them. Think of the many rich characters you see in the movies. They're often portrayed as evil, cruel villains. We grow up watching these shows on TV and begin to associate wealth and abundance with bad behavior. Since most of us don't want to be like that, we can develop a mindset around this that imposes limits on our own abundance.

A mindset is established when the conscious mind and the subconscious become one. *"Therefore, shall a man leave his father and his mother, and shall cleave unto his wife: and the two shall become one flesh"* (Genesis 2:24). Here we have another allegory. Obviously, husband and wife don't literally become one flesh, so we know this is describing something else.

I remember hearing over and over when I was growing up that money is the root of all evil, and the funny thing is, that's not what the Bible says. It says, *"The love of money is the root of all evil"* (1 Timothy 6:10). What this verse means is that the love of money above everything else in life is "the root of all evil." When we vigorously pursue money above everything else in our lives—friends, family, love—this is not good. When the balance is tipped, and we have made money too important in our lives, we begin to serve money rather than allowing money to serve us.

As previously mentioned, the ego is a false self that tries to protect us by saying things like, "We better not buy that new outfit. We may need the money for something else," or "We really can't afford to help that person out, we may need the money for ourselves." Have you ever experienced this? These thoughts are simply products of the poverty mindset. They don't belong to you. They're not yours. It's the ego talking. It really helps if we can put some space between the ego and our true God-Self and see the ego as the facade that it is. There are meditations at the end of the chapter to help us let go of the ego.

The Apostle Paul struggled with the ego conundrum as well. Check out what he says here: *"I do not understand what I do. For what I want to do, I do not do, but what I hate I do"* (Romans 7:15 NIV). Paul is talking about his true Self wrestling with his false self (ego). His higher Self wants to do things one way, and his ego wants him to do things differently. We can apply this to our own lives; our true Self wants and desires an abundant life, but our false self (ego) often wants to keep us locked inside our familiar thought patterns or mindset because it is fearful of change because then it has to give up part of its assumed false identity.

"The spirit indeed is willing, but the flesh is weak." (Matthew 26:41)

The poverty mindset is not who we are. It is an imposter. Our true Self would never identify as being unworthy or undeserving of living an abundant life. We need to be honest with ourselves. Do we have a hard time spending money, especially on ourselves? Do we have a hard time letting money leave our hands in general? Why would this be? Are we afraid that it might not come back to us? Do we get frustrated when paying our bills? When an unexpected expense arises, do we have a meltdown as if it were the end of the world? Do we look at wealthy people in a negative way? This is not the energy of abundance—it's the energy of a poverty mentality, and no matter how enlightened we may become, it can and will rear its ugly head from time to time.

So, what is the energy of abundance? The energy of abundance is positive, producing a feeling of peaceful relief. If you were to receive a large amount of money, your financial stress would fade away, and you would feel a sense of relief knowing that you didn't need to worry about finances anymore. You would relax because money would no longer be an issue. You would feel the freedom that financial security provides. Use your imagination right now. Take a moment and imagine what it would feel like to be independently wealthy. Take a deep breath and feel the relief. Feel the freedom. Sit with this for as long as you wish, memorize this feeling, and return to it whenever you are stressed about money. This simple technique can work wonders for you. Feeling is the secret, and when you drop into this feeling, you are signaling to the subconscious mind that you are living an abundant life. This positive re-imagining chips away at the poverty mindset.

An amazing New Thought teacher named Florence Scovel Shinn wrote a book published in 1925 called *The Game of Life and How to Play It*. In this book, she describes the use of affirmations as the number one way to alleviate the poverty mindset. She prescribed an affirmation of abundance to use every time we spend money regardless of the situation: "God is my endless supply. It cannot be depleted. As money goes out, immediately money comes back in, under grace in perfect ways."

"Thou shalt also decree a thing, and it shall be established unto thee: and the light shall shine upon thy ways." (Job 22:28)

The definition of decree is an official order issued by a legal authority (Oxford Dictionary). As God in the flesh, we are the legal authority of our reality, so let us decree that by God's grace, we have the power through our imagination to create our abundant reality, and we will see it established in our lives. May the light of abundance shine upon us!

Using *Reality Is Negotiable* as our guide, we can manifest the abundant life that we truly desire. When it arrives, we will be able to enjoy it to the fullest and not walk around with Imposter Syndrome, feeling like we don't deserve it. The truth is, regardless of what the ego may tell us, we are the I AM.

MEDITATION FOR TWO: LOVE AND LET GO
Duration: 25 Minutes/Session
(WILL LIKELY TAKE MANY SESSIONS)

This meditation is designed for couples in a committed relationship. Below the first meditation, you will find a variation designed for the individual. Both are equally effective.

Find a quiet place where you will not be disturbed for the next 25 minutes or so. If appropriate, dim the lights and light a candle. Sit across from each other comfortably, either on the floor with meditation cushions or in chairs (whichever you prefer). Both you and your partner join hands.

Gaze into each other's eyes for several minutes. Feel the energy flowing in and around and through the two of you. It is here in this sacred space that you acknowledge the one love that you share with each other. It is mystical and unique, and it belongs only to you. Looking into each other's eyes, feel the warming sensation washing over you as your souls make contact. It is now that your higher selves can safely reveal to you any energy blocks that have been hindering your joint creations.

Continuing to gaze into each other's eyes, become aware of the mutual egoic self that you both share in this relationship. Hold space for this form—it is your joint creation. Acknowledge and feel it as being separate from you, hovering above the two of you. This egoic self is not the real you, though it has been with you for some time. All its fears, all its doubts, all its anxieties do not belong to the two of you. It has only tried to shield you from the real world and keep you from being hurt, and in doing so, it has negated your mutual creative energy, blocking the flow of abundance into the life you share.

Now, close your eyes, and in a quiet voice say together: "We acknowledge you and thank you for all you have tried to do for us, but your services are no longer needed. You are dismissed." Sit quietly with your eyes closed, holding hands as the form dissipates above you. Take a slow deep, relaxing breath, and as you exhale, slowly open your eyes and say to each other: "It is done."

Abundance is now. It is yours. Walk together into your new life free and untethered from the ego, knowing that *"all the old things have passed away, and everything has become new"* (2 Cor. 5:17, paraphrased).

INDIVIDUAL VARIATION: LOVE AND LET GO

Duration: 10-15 Minutes/Session

(WILL LIKELY TAKE MANY SESSIONS)

This meditation involves using a mirror, so the bathroom is a common place to do this; however, if you have a mirror that you can set in front of you, any space will do. You can do this at any time, sitting or standing.

Stand or sit in front of a mirror and gaze at your reflection. Look deeply into your eyes for a few minutes. Feel compassion for the one in the mirror, acknowledging their hardships, shortcomings, and sufferings. There is no criticism or judgment towards this reflection, only love. Say to your reflection: "I love you." Now, gently close your eyes and be still and quiet for a few minutes. Acknowledge the presence of your egoic self, become aware and sense that it is something separate from you, hovering between you and your reflection. All the fears, all the doubts, all the anxiety do not belong to you—they are not yours. They belong to this form. These emotions have blocked your creative energy and prevented abundance from flowing into your life.

In a quiet voice, with eyes closed, say the words: "I acknowledge and thank you for always being there, but your services are no longer required. You are dismissed." Be still and quiet for a few minutes as the form dissipates in front of you. Take a deep, slow, relaxing breath, and when you are ready, slowly open your eyes. Look at your reflection and say the words: "It is done."

You are now free. Abundance is yours. Step into your new life knowing that *"old things have passed away, and all things have become new"* (2 Cor. 5:17, paraphrased).

"What seems to be, is, to those to whom it seems to be, and is productive of the most dreadful consequences, to those to whom it seems to be, even of torments, despair and eternal death."

- William Blake

CHAPTER 16

DWELLER ON THE THRESHOLD

As mentioned earlier, negotiating reality is not all wine and roses. We will have challenges, but if we are going to live like the God we are, we should see these times as opportunities rather than obstacles.

"I have told you these things, so that in me you may have peace. In this world you will have trouble. But take heart! I have overcome the world." (John 16:33 NIV)

This is one the most comforting and reassuring verses in all of scripture, and it reveals the biggest secret of reality creation. We humans want everything to be perfect, but reality doesn't work that way. At the highest level of consciousness, sure, but down here in our dense 3D world, if we expect everything to be perfect all the time, we're setting ourselves up for disappointment and failure...nevertheless, we desire perfection anyway.

When we see successful spiritual people on social media platforms, our ego immediately engages. We see them on the screen, and it appears as though their lives are a cakewalk. We presume that if we were as spiritually adept as they are, nothing in life would ever go wrong. This is not the case, and they would be the first to tell you that they deal with the same difficult times as everyone else.

The secret lies in knowing that we will have trouble in this world, and by knowing this, we won't be caught off guard when it comes. The verse on the previous page instructs us to take heart during these times because whatever trouble we're dealing with has already been overcome. This shows us the big picture, the now, where everything is happening everywhere. We experience trouble, and at the same time, we have overcome it. If you can embed this truth in your subconscious mind, then you can have peace in the midst of any storm.

There's no doubt that troubling circumstances can be challenging, but if we know we have already overcome them, we can look at these times as opportunities rather than obstacles. Life's challenges serve a higher purpose, although it's not always easy to see that. Without these challenges, we would never grow in consciousness. And we came here to learn and grow.

Each of us has tailor made challenges that are presented along our spiritual path. We are all different, but we are one, and no matter what it may seem like at the time, we are never facing a challenge alone. We are one body with many parts, and whatever challenges we as individuals may face, once the challenge is overcome it serves to benefit the whole. When one of us overcomes a challenge, it moves the whole of humanity forward.

It can be a great comfort for us here and now to know that our higher Self has already overcome our current challenges—or we could say our future Self has already overcome our present problems. This may be hard to wrap your head around, but knowing this truth will help boost your confidence in negotiating your own reality. You are an overcomer, and no matter your current situation, you will overcome it. Take the verse on page 221 (John 16:33) as if it were written directly to you from your future Self. Take heart, and know that this too shall pass.

Now that you are armed with the necessary knowledge to negotiate reality, we need to talk about one final esoteric challenge that we all must face at some point on our individual spiritual journeys. This is known as confronting "The Dweller on the Threshold."

This challenge is presented to us once we consciously decide to seek out our own spiritual truth regardless of any consequences or religious fallout we might endure. There's no looking back because we are on a mission of awakening, and we won't be deterred.

Just as we arrive at the threshold of enlightenment, the Dweller appears. The Dweller on the Threshold is a metaphysical manifestation of your lower self whose sole purpose is to keep you from stepping across the threshold to spiritual freedom. Its role is to try and get you to believe that the truth you seek is a lie and that it would be best for you to settle back into your old belief system. This can get ugly, especially if you have a church background with many years of having had damaging ideas planted in your head about a God outside of yourself.

The Dweller can appear in many spiritual and physical forms, but no matter what form it takes, it will be specially designed just for you. You will know when you have this encounter because you will feel like you are so close to the truth you seek, and out of nowhere something will come that tries to knock you off course. I can't tell you what this will be because it is different for everyone. However, I know it will be painfully personal, and you will feel it like a sucker punch to your gut from the great unknown.

As William Blake said, "What seems to be, is, to those to whom it seems to be." Yep, the good ol' Dweller on the Threshold lives in the world of "what seems to be." He/she/they/it is a monster of our own making, a mental creation of limited beliefs, low-level consciousness, and negative thought patterns—and since thoughts become reality, this thing appears to us right before our very eyes.

Limiting beliefs...we all have them. The Dweller on the Threshold is the embodiment of our most supreme limiting beliefs. You know, the dominant ones that take precedence over all the others, the ones that keep us from feeling free, and just when we are on the cusp of a true spiritual awakening, this monster appears. I wish I could give you more of a detailed description of what this will look like for you, but I can share my personal experience with the Dweller so when yours appears, you will recognize it for what it is. This is key, because if we do not recognize it when it approaches our threshold, it may very well succeed in keeping us from our awakening.

I was absolutely stupefied when the Dweller appeared in my physical reality. It happened at a busy gas station in Tulsa, Oklahoma, of all places! Let me give you a little background so that you can grasp the heaviness of this situation.

I grew up in a strict Christian household, and I was a young boy during the famous "Satanic Panic" that began in the 1980s. It was bad. My parents were so scared that we might end up in hell one day that they took me out in the backyard and made me burn all of my rock and roll records. Sinful music like the Beatles and Van Halen. It seems ridiculous looking back, yes, but it took its toll on me. Before long, I was scared to death that I might commit some unforgivable sin and end up burning in a lake of fire for all eternity—what a nice way to grow up. This stuff gets lodged in your subconscious as a kid, and it compounds and multiplies as you get older. No matter what you do, you always have this looming fear of hell in the back of your mind.

I spent pretty much my whole childhood in church, trying my best to please God. As I grew older, I began to explore other religions and cultures, but I still always claimed myself to be Christian. I eventually ended up becoming an international missionary in India, sharing the so-called "good news" with thousands upon thousands of people.

After spending several years working in Christian ministry, I started to spiritually awaken and realized that these beliefs I had held since childhood were simply no longer serving me and had, in fact, never served me. The dogma the Church was teaching no longer resonated with me in any way, shape, or form. I knew in my heart that there was more to this whole God thing than they were letting on.

Around this time, as mentioned earlier in the book, I had concluded that if God is love, then there is no way there could be a place called hell. This understanding led me to the realization that I, along with every other human being, is simply God expressing his/her/their Self in these individualized forms.

I meditated on this and felt it to be true—and yet, after all these years, that nagging false belief from childhood would still rear up ferociously on occasion. When this happened, it caused deep internal anxiety, like a battle for truth raging in my head. "What if my new beliefs and what I'm feeling is wrong?" I asked myself, and the ego would subtly remind me that if I'm wrong, I may end up in hell, separated from God. This is a miserable state of mind to be trapped in, and I'm convinced that it can drive a person insane if left unchecked, all thanks to the toxic fallacies about God that the Church taught us as children and continues to preach to this day.

It was during this time of opening to new spiritual thought and seriously questioning my old beliefs that the Dweller on the Threshold appeared to me right at the crux of awakening as God. On this particular morning, I felt an unexplained sadness, anger, and a visceral sense of impending doom. This made no logical sense. The day before, I was ecstatic with spiritual joy and genuine happiness. I now had a real sense that everything I had been experiencing and learning recently was wrong, that it was all made-up "woo-woo" nonsense. I had a suspicious feeling that none of it was true, that I was on the wrong path. Despite how much I had grown spiritually and how genuine and true everything was resonating with me, at that moment, I was feeling overwhelmed with discouragement and confusion. It seemed to have come out of nowhere, trying to drag me back into my former church-affiliated beliefs.

I went about my day being rather irritable toward my family—not mean, but distant and agitated. A battle of new thoughts versus old thoughts raged inside my mind. Miserable, I could feel myself being pulled into the fog of disillusionment. It was strong, it was scary, and I felt like I might be going crazy.

I left the house, got in my truck and went to work. I had a few clients to tend to that day, so I was going to put on a fake smile and make it happen. I was so upset that this newfound peace of mind and way of life was now in limbo. It was deeply frustrating. On my way to work, I pulled into a gas station to fill up my truck and grab a cup of coffee. Little did I know the Dweller on the Threshold was breathing down my neck.

I pulled up to pump #7 and sat in my truck, contemplating everything swirling in my mind for several minutes. I was thinking about knowing I am God, and yet, at the same time feeling like this was wrong and blasphemous. I felt like I was being torn in half. I cannot overstate how horrific this was—the struggle was very real. Suddenly, I hear someone yelling.

This was a very large gas station at a very busy intersection, and it was swarming with customers. As I sat at pump #7, I could hear someone yelling at the top of their lungs. I rolled down the window and looked around. Trying to determine where all the yelling was coming from, I saw two guys standing at the intersection. One of them is holding a sign that says, "God is love. Please repent," and the other one is looking right at me and yelling, "God is judging you because you think you are God!"

At that moment, my ego told me that this was confirmation that I was on the wrong spiritual path. Frozen in my seat, its voice was strong and hard to resist. Yet, the new me, the free me, the God me, the real me, knew otherwise. This was the Dweller on the Threshold, and its tactic was shockingly scary, very real, and above all else deeply personal.

The Dweller was manifesting in my physical reality as a last-ditch effort to pull me back into my religious past and prevent me from living a life of freedom in my loving self-awareness of God.

At this point in my life, I was only vaguely aware of this phenomenon known as the Dweller on the Threshold. There were only two instances where I had ever heard of this. One was from a podcast called the *Duncan Trussell Family Hour*. The host of the podcast, Duncan Trussell, had been interviewing a spiritual teacher, and during their conversation, he began to describe his personal encounter with the Dweller along his path to enlightenment. The other time was during a Neville Goddard lecture entitled "The Dweller On the Threshold" from 1971, so I didn't have a good understanding then of what I was experiencing.

As I mentioned earlier, the Dweller on the Threshold is a conglomeration of our sinful egoic thoughts, actions, words and beliefs. "Sinful" means the thoughts that have caused us to miss the mark of what we were aiming for. I was aiming to awaken to my true Self, and I was almost there. I was so close that I could feel it, about to cross over the threshold into complete spiritual freedom, and then the Dweller appeared and threw every deep, dark doubt at me that it possibly could. It even manifested into a curbside evangelist at a local gas station, yelling at me the exact things that I was wrestling with inside my head.

After the initial sinking feeling wore off, I couldn't help but crack a smile. I had been vaguely aware of the concept of the Dweller on the Threshold, and just that slight awareness allowed the space for me to push forward through the confusion, and surprisingly, I began to feel a sense of oneness with the gas station preacher. Then the most beautiful synchronicity happened.

I walked into the gas station, grabbed my cup of coffee, and filled my truck up with gas. Right before I took off, I opened Spotify and hit the random play button. Seemingly out of nowhere, a randomly generated song by Van Morrison began to play, called "The Dweller on the Threshold." I had never even heard of this song before, and I sat there in utter bewilderment, marveling as this beautiful music caressed my mind and spirit—as if he was singing to my very soul. I even felt tears of joy track down my cheeks as I played this song over and over again. Coming at the perfect time, this synchronicity was a gift from the universe that I will cherish for the rest of my life.

"Then the glory of the Lord went up from the cherub, and stood over the threshold of the house; and the house was filled with the cloud, and the court was filled with the brightness of the Lord's glory." (Ezekiel 10:4)

This verse is a spiritual representation of what's going on behind the scenes during these types of experiences in our physical 3D reality. When we are at the threshold of enlightenment, the Cloud is there with us, offering its perfect knowledge of the situation. The whole scene shines with the brightness of our divine nature, our true Self, as we step into our destiny as the God we truly are.

This concept may seem a little far-fetched to talk about, but it shouldn't be. We all must face the Dweller at some point along our spiritual path, and having this knowledge will keep us from setbacks when we encounter this common spiritual phenomenon. *"My people are destroyed for lack of knowledge"* (Hosea 4:6).

The Dweller on the Threshold is highly individualized for each of us because it is, in fact, us—a manifestation of our shadow side. There is a lot of discussion these days on shadow work, and the gist of it is non-resistance; in other words, not denying that this darker side of us exists. Herein lies a clue for how we should handle the Dweller experience when it presents itself to us.

Some people have had this experience in a dream, some have had a vision, and some have experienced it through the use of psychedelics. There are a myriad of ways one may encounter the Dweller on the Threshold, but rest assured, we will all have this experience in some fashion along our journey to enlightenment.

When we encounter the Dweller, we have two options. One, which it's banking on, is to shrink back in fear and assume our old limiting beliefs, our wrong thought patterns, and in essence, become the old familiar self again. The Dweller's only aim is to derail us from our current path of awakening. Many people choose this option because it's a lot less scary than venturing across the threshold into unknown territory. However, while it may seem like the safest option at the time, it ultimately leads to an unfulfilled life. The truth is we are simply choosing which part of ourselves we want to identify with.

So, if we don't choose option number one, the only other option is to fight, but not in the way you may think. The Dweller on the Threshold is the embodiment of your greatest doubts, and it must be defeated if you are going to advance. Here's the kicker: you defeat this sinful beast, your own dark shadow monster, by acknowledging it and embracing it. It can only be defeated with pure love. Whatever form it may take, embrace it with love. Acknowledge its existence, how it has always been there, and how it is no longer serving you.

This is your shadow, and you must smother this side of you with love, compassion, and understanding. Stay with this love, no matter how long the Dweller fights. Before long, this horrible monstrosity will have no choice but to dissolve into the love that you have for yourself, and when it does, you will be made whole and walk effortlessly across the threshold. You will not be turned away. You will cross the threshold into the land of spiritual freedom.

The entire world and everything in it is ourselves pushed out. We are God, and we are playing all the parts. As within, so without. It's all in our heads, including the Dweller on the Threshold. It is both real and not real at the same time; it is and it isn't; and this is the nature of life, the reality in which we choose to live our truth.

SHADOW LOVE, A THOUGHT EXERCISE

This exercise will help prepare you as you approach the threshold of awakening. Reflect on those parts of yourself that you are not proud of, but instead of feeling ashamed, have compassion on those aspects of your life.

Love yourself unconditionally. Imagine a large, elegant, handwoven tapestry. There are many different colored threads running through it, some are light-colored, and some are dark-colored, but all of them are woven together to form something unique and beautiful. If you pulled out all the dark threads, the whole thing wouldn't look right before it started to unravel. Picture your entire life as a big, beautiful tapestry made in love, light and dark threads alike.

You can and should use the divine power of your imagination to create an ideal reality for yourself. But the endgame of negotiating reality is not just to secure the prize. When on an airplane, you are advised if there is a threat of crashing to first put on your own oxygen mask and then you can help other passengers. Be personally convinced that you are the I AM—God of the universe—then go out and make this world a better place.

"And God said, let there be_______________."

... you decide.

In conclusion, I'm reminded of a time several years ago when I was hiking the Appalachian Trail, a path which spans 2,190 miles from Georgia to Maine. My friend and I were on a section of the trail known as the "Hogpen Gap" in the mountains of northern Georgia when we came upon a handmade log shelter. Inside was a wooden bench, and on this bench were various items and supplies left by other hikers who had come before us. This is known in the hiking world as "Trail Magic." There were a few bottles of water, several granola bars, some peanuts, a few pairs of socks, a blanket, a map, some paperback books, and a couple of hiking sticks. On the shelter's wall, just above the bench, was a handwritten note that said, "Keep going. You're on the right path. Take what you need. Leave what you don't."

This is my offering to you: "Trail Magic" on your spiritual journey. As Ram Dass said, "We're all just walking each other home."

ACKNOWLEDGEMENTS

I am eternally grateful to the high-vibe tribe at Namaste Publishing. Your talent and commitment to bring life-changing books to the world are a thing of beauty! Thank you for all that you have done to bring *Reality Is Negotiable* to press. It's an absolute honor to be in partnership with you!

A huge shout out to my son, Dayden Yarnell, for designing the awesome artwork for this book. You never cease to amaze me!

Of course, none of this would be possible without the amazing love and support of my wife, Tina. Our early morning deep dives into the things of God are my inspiration, and I'm so thankful that I have you at my side!

To our children, I think it's so cool that we get to experience life together. You are my true gurus!

And finally, a shout out to William Blake, a kindred spirit from a far-off century, who understood that the Bible was addressed to the human imagination and expressed his own revelation through his poetry and art.

ABOUT THE AUTHOR

Justin Yarnell is a Christian mystic, biblical scholar, spiritual teacher, author and counsellor. After spending over 20 years in the mainstream Christian faith and working full-time in ministry at one of America's largest churches, he experienced a personal awakening. After this experience, he could no longer remain plugged into the megachurch culture in the U.S., so he chose to leave organized religion altogether and began his unique spiritual journey.

He has never looked back.

Justin found his niche along the spiritual path, helping people transition from Church life to authentic spiritual freedom.

Justin remains an ordained minister but is not associated with any faith, church or religion. His passion is helping people transform their lives by renewing their minds to authentic spiritual truths.

He resides in the USA with his wife and children.

books that change your life

Our Publishing Mission is to make available healing and transformational publications that acknowledge, celebrate, and encourage our readers to live from their true essence and thereby come to remember who they truly are.